INTRODUCTION

THANK YOU… for purchasing a copy of my sec...
Truly Madly Healthy Free From Re...

It was in May 2011 when I first had the idea to write a cook book and with a lot of cooking, tasting, feeding my friends and family, and of course washing up, I am delighted to finish my second book!

I was overwhelmed with the positive response that my first book received. The book achieved exactly what I wanted it to–Making Healthy Meals taste delicious and nutritious.

Since then I have continued to study and learn, bake, roast and cook so I can bring you the most up to date and practical advice to keep you all healthy.

KEEP THE TREATS
Treats don't have to be packed with things you are trying to avoid. Super Healthy Snacks and Treats, by Jenna Zoe (Ryland Peters & Small, £15), and Truly Madly Healthy, by Jemma Govier (£20), will satisfy the pickiest sweet tooth.
189

Since my last book, TMH has been going from strength to strength and we now even have our own TMH Pure Protein Powder.

A highlight from my first book is that it was mentioned in Vogue's New Year Health Trends by Calgary Avansino.

TMH Free From Recipes book comes with my same dream to keep creating healthy and delicious simple meals that you can all recreate in your own kitchens!

Today's Nutrition
TRULY MADLY HEALTHY
For Tomorrow's Health

For the past six years I have been a Full Time Personal Trainer running my Bootcamp Business, and spending any spare minute creating new recipes in our Kitchen. Over this time my hobby for cooking has evolved into my daily passion. Cooking for me is a way to celebrate, relax, bring people together and enjoy life!

After training and teaching many women over this time, I now specialise in Female Fat Loss. I practice all my advice first to ensure that I am passing on practical advise that I truly believe. My aim is for any client (and you) is to make your life simpler!

I want to pass on my knowledge from my experiences, so you know exactly what works. You will then have honest and practical advice to help you recreate the delicious dishes at home.

We have also had a great time at **TMH** running our **Supper Clubs**. These have been a brilliant way to test out all my new recipes in a fun and relaxed way.

In my first book I gave you my Top Tips and here are my revised Top Tips to help you live the 'TMH Way'

❦TMH Top Tips

1. Eat protein with breakfast, lunch and dinner. Yes if you have my first book then this will look familiar because it is something that works, so why would I change it! Complete Protein is all meat, fish and eggs and I always recommend organic protein. This is number one for a reason, I have seen hundreds of food diaries over the years and the people with the very best results have one main thing in common, they all eat high quality protein at each meal. If you are vegan or vegetarian then I recommend a high quality vegan protein shake, nuts, seeds, legumes, pulses, hemp and lots of vegetables to increase your protein intake.

2. Eliminate all the inflammatory foods. These foods are linked with causing disease and you will feel better for removing them. Gluten, wheat, artificial sugars and sweeteners, aspartame, alcohol and processed dairy.

3. Don't think that by skipping meals means you can now have a glass of wine later as not all calories are equal. Talking of empty calories, if you drink fizzy drinks, I recommend you stop. Diet drinks are full of aspartame, a chemical sugar, which makes you hungrier and end up putting on more weight. In other words, as far as "sweetness satisfaction" in the...

More TMH Top Tips

3. (continued) human brain is concerned, your brain can tell the difference between a real sugar and an artificial one, even if your conscious mind cannot. So you continue to crave more and more sweetness, in the form of diet drinks, sugar or whatever sweet treats you can find.

4. We are all different! This is what makes us unique so we can't then expect to all need the exact same amount of foods as somebody else. What works for one person may not work for you. However, what I do know is that eliminating the processed foods is good for all of us. So listen to your body and learn what it gets on well with. For example if you had a high fat breakfast, eggs, salmon and avocado, are you full up or are you still hungry? Listen to your body and it will tell you what it needs.

5. Find a balance. For me it is eating super clean and healthy in the week, then I relax on a Saturday night. This means I can look forward to a treat meal with friends and family without any guilt. I don't have to say I am "back on it" when Monday morning comes around again as I haven't ruined all my hard work. There really is no quick fix, it is being consistent all the time.

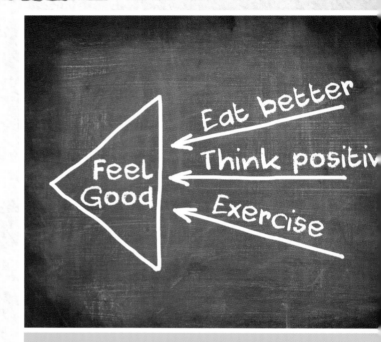

Feel Good — Eat better — Think positiv — Exercise

WE ARE ALL DIFFERENT!

HEALTHY
BODY MIND SPIRIT

6. Talking about no quick fixes! I have worked with thousands of people through **TMH** recipes or in a corporate environment and one of the biggest things I have learnt is you have to make daily significant changes and keep to them. It is no good, sticking to a plan for, 7 days or 6 weeks if you are then just going to go back to your old habits. I have heard some people say "I can't wait to get back to eating normally", what is normally, eating foods that are processed, convenient and loaded with rubbish? You need to focus on changing daily new habits to make them ever lasting. They have to be automatic habits like getting up and brushing your teeth!

7. Don't swap one sugar for another. Yes I recommend using Raw Honey and dates as a far more natural source of sugars but remember they still raise your blood sugar levels and should be used in a varied diet. My favorite sugar alternative is Stevia as it is from a plant so it doesn't raise our blood sugar levels like other sugars and sweeteners. See my Sugar list on the following page!!!

8. Get your mind right. If you are telling yourself that "I don't enjoy eating healthily, I wish I could eat some cake right now" then all you are doing is creating negative feelings around these habits. Look on the bright side, you are fuelling your precious body with the nutrients and vitamins that it needs to THRIVE!

9. Know what you want and go for it! I have found that the clients who achieve the best results are the ones who set goals and stay focused. Even if it takes longer than you want, as long as you have that same goal in mind. I stay on track by pushing myself, either to become stronger in the gym, enter a running event, Tough Mudder competition or even just looking good on holiday in a bikini. It keeps me on track and keeps my hand out of the biscuit tin!!

10. Live it everyday! These changes need to be consistent and forever as this isn't a diet. This is a new healthy way of living, back to cooking with healthy ingredients and looking after your body.

SUGAR-NO LIST

THE TRUTH ABOUT SUGAR...

So is all sugar the same? Well in a word... No! Dr Mercola summed them all up perfectly, so here is a simple list so you have the knowledge to choose which ones to avoid.

Dextrose, **fructose**, and **glucose** are all monosaccharides, known as simple sugars. The primary difference between them is how your body metabolises them. Glucose and dextrose are essentially the same sugar. However, food manufacturers usually use the term "dextrose" in their ingredient list. Fructose is found in fruit.

The simple sugars can combine to form more complex sugars, like the *disaccharide* sucrose (table sugar), which is half glucose and half fructose.

High fructose corn syrup (HFCS) is 55 percent fructose and 45 percent glucose.

Ethanol (drinking alcohol) is not a sugar, although beer and wine contain residual sugars and starches, in addition to alcohol.

Sugar alcohols like xylitol, glycerol, sorbitol, maltitol, mannitol, and erythritol are neither sugars nor alcohols but are becoming increasingly popular as sweeteners. They are incompletely absorbed by your small intestine, for the most part, so they provide fewer calories than sugar but often cause problems with bloating, diarrhea, and flatulence.

Sucralose (Splenda) is NOT a sugar, despite its sugar-like name and deceptive marketing slogan, "made from sugar." It's a chlorinated artificial sweetener in line with *aspartame* and saccharin, with detrimental health effects to match.

Agave syrup, falsely advertised as "natural," is typically HIGHLY processed and is usually *80 percent fructose*. The end product does not even remotely resemble the original agave plant. This has changed my mind on this product!

YES LIST

DATES

The benefits of dates include relief from constipation, intestinal disorders, heart problems, anaemia, sexual dysfunction, diarrhoea, abdominal cancer, and many other conditions. **Dates** are high in natural sugars like glucose, fructose, and sucrose. Therefore, they are the perfect snack for an immediate burst of energy.

TMH tips Dates are often categorized as a laxative food.

TMH tips Make your own Date Syrup by dicing dates, adding to a pan with 250ml of water and heat over a medium heat until it becomes sticky, then mash with a fork. Once most of the water is absorbed you can add to a blender if you want it smoother.

HONEY

Honey is about 53 percent fructose, but is completely natural in its raw form and has many health benefits when used in moderation, including as many antioxidants as spinach.

STEVIA

Stevia is a highly sweet herb derived from the leaf of the South American stevia plant, which is completely safe (in its natural form). This is why we use it in our **TMH Pure Protein Powder**.

Lo han (or luohanguo) is another natural sweetener, but derived from a fruit.

This is a little more than just a Cook Book!! Well a lot more really!!

The more I study and learn the more I want to pass it on to you, so here are some of my top TMH Health Body & Home Tips.

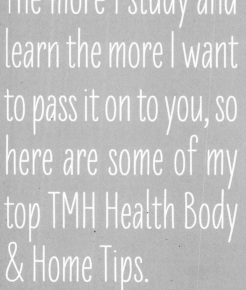

All you need is love

STOCK UP LIST

Once you have the following ingredients in your larder then you will be good to go.

Coconut Oil

Coconut Oil is a delicious oil extracted from the kernel or meat of matured coconuts harvested from the coconut palm (Cocos nucifera). It has various applications in food, medicine, and industry. Because of its high saturated fat content it is slow to oxidize, which makes it perfect for cooking under heat. There are hundreds of health benefits of coconut oil, here are just a small few:

- Taken for a natural energy boost
- As a coffee creamer when emulsified into coffee
- On the skin as a basic lotion
- To support a Healthy Thyroid Function
- Help boost your Metabolism
- As an eye-makeup remover
- Use as a nourishing hair mask
- To lighten age spots when rubbed directly on the skin
- To prevent stretch marks during pregnancy

2 Chia Seeds

The chia seed was used as part of a staple diet in South America and has now been rediscovered and made its way into Europe. It is known as a "superfood" and a "runners food", due to its concentrated amounts of polyunsaturated omega-3 fatty acid, fibre, protein and minerals.

Milk Facts

The path that transforms healthy milk products into allergens and carcinogens begins with modern feeding methods that substitute high-protein, soy-based feeds for fresh green grass and breeding methods to produce cows with abnormally large pituitary glands so that they produce three times more milk than the old fashioned scrub cow. These cows need antibiotics to keep them well.

Their milk is then pasteurised so that all valuable enzymes are destroyed (lactase for the assimilation of lactose; galactase for the assimilation of galactose; phosphatase for the assimilation of calcium.

Literally dozens of other precious enzymes are destroyed in the pasterisation process. Without them, milk is very difficult to digest. The human pancreas is not always able to produce these enzymes; over-stress of the pancreas can lead to diabetes and other diseases).

"Cow's milk is the number one allergic food in this country. It has been well documented as a cause in diarrhea, cramps, bloating, gas, gastrointestinal bleeding, iron-deficiency anaemia, skin rashes, atherosclerosis, and acne.

It is the primary cause of recurrent ear infections in children. It has also been linked to insulin dependent diabetes, rheumatoid arthritis, infertility and leukemia."

Dr Mercola

Alternatives to Dairy

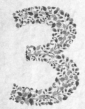

3 Almond Milk Unsweetened

Almond milk is a plant-based alternative to traditional dairy milk. Almond milk is made by toasting and grinding almonds and then blending them with filtered water. Almond milk does not contain any dairy, lactose, soy, eggs, cholesterol, gluten, MSG, or casein or whey. Take a look in the Drinks section to find out how to make your own.

Coconut Milk Unsweetened

Coconut flesh (the white part) is grated and soaked in hot water. The coconut cream rises to the top and can be skimmed off. The remaining liquid is squeezed through a cheesecloth to extract a white liquid that is coconut milk. By repeating this process, the coconut milk becomes thinner. The thicker version is used for desserts and rich sauces.

 TMH tips Did you know that Coconut is fruit and not a nut!!

Good Organic Brands

Lets do Organic—from Amazon

Avoid the tinned ones

"A potential problem with canned coconut milk is guar gum. Guar gum is a galactomannan, which is a polysaccharide consisting of a mannose backbone with a galactose side group. It's primarily the endosperm of guar beans which lots of people find hard to digest."

Chris Kresser

 Nut Butters

These are just spread like Peanut butters, but I personally favour them over peanuts as they are one of a several crops that are vulnerable to aflatoxins, toxins produced by fungi that grow in or on certain foods and feeds. I love Almond, hazelnut and cashew, and you can find them in health stores and lots of supermarkets aisles, with the peanut butter.

Apple Cider Vinegar

Real organic apple cider vinegar, is made by fermenting pressed apple juice until the sugars turn to vinegar. Importantly, it should be made from organic apples and be unheated, unfiltered and unpasterised. This is the cloudiness colour that you are looking for. It can help strengthen your immune system, prevent candida, help regulate blood sugar levels, detox and so much more.

Natural Nourishing Traditions

So a great man once said, that women and men's hormones are like this, a woman's are like a finely tuned Ferrari and man's is like a dump truck! So ladies to help you tune into the complex world of hormones, here are some helpful facts from pre and post menopause!

So why is a cook book talking about Hormones, I hear you ask ? Well you can only truly be healthy if all of your body is working in harmony together, and your hormones are absolutely vital.

From the age of 35 fewer cycles occur and there is a subsequent decline in progesterone (a hormone). The reason the following areas of the body are

affected is because they are progesterone receptor sites: Brain (our moods) Skin (hot flushes) Breast (soreness) Adrenal glands and uterus. It can be a stressful time for the body so here are my helpful tips.

Celery is proven to be a relaxing food and can help with cooling the body down and cleansing.

Adaptogens are herbs that help to reduce stress on the body. They're called adaptogens because of their unique ability to "adapt" their function according to your body's specific needs.

Ginseng – Ashwaganda – Rhodiola – Cordyce Muchrooms – Reishi & Shitake Mushrooms – Goji Beiires – Maca powder

Liquorice

Liquorice (not the sweet kind) has been shown to treat chronic fatigue, digestive and liver disorders and it is great at helping clearing mucus. I recommend you take it first thing with grapefruit juice.

Green tea

Can be used to improve alertness as it contains L-Theanine. It does contain caffeine so should not be used in excess.

The healthier your gut, the flatter your tummy! Sea Vegetables–Kombu–Kelp–Wakame–Chlorella.

These are cleansing Japanese sea vegetables as they are high in iodine so can help people with hypothyroidism. .They are like little sponges that attract the goodness and toxins, so it is essential to get yours from a non toxic water source. They have been shown to modulate oestrogen in Japanese postmenopausal women.

Soya–The Healthy way! Miso–Check out my Miso Soup.

Probiotic Foods–The Natural Way

These foods all contain natural occurring probiotics to help support good bacteria in the gut.

For the geeks like me–Lacto-fermentation really is more art than science. The science part is simple: lactobacillus (from a prepared culture, fresh whey, or just naturally occurring) plus sugar (naturally present in vegetables and fruits), plus a little salt, minus oxygen (anaerobic process), plus time, equal lactic acid fermentation. The ideal temperature is around 22 degrees, but warmer or cooler temperature will still work. You can buy kits online and start your own at home!

LACTOFERMENTED FOODS

Yoghurt–Dairy (Raw, Organic)

Kefir–Dairy

Sauerkraut–Vegetable

Kimchi–Vegetable

Omebushi Plum–Fruit

Kombucha–Tea

Kefir

IMPROVING MINERAL BIOAVAILABILITY
AKA Getting more out of your food!!

Soaking Nuts, Seeds and Pulses

In a Nut Shell (sorry bad joke) what the soaking does is deactivates the lectins in the pulses or nuts etc which then softens them leaving them far easier for us to be able to digest. Soaking them in warm water is more effective at reducing the phytic acid than cold water.

 I recommend soaking them in warm water with sea salt.

Souring foods can be achieved by using lemon juice, apple cider vinegar (1 tsp per cup) yoghurt, kefir or whey.

Bone Broth

Which just means a slow cooking process using the entire meat and bones.

Collagen, Gelatin, Glutamine and Glycine are just some of the amino acids that can all help protect the gut lining. Helps regenerate cartilage and heal joints, helps with food allergies and has many more benefits.

 Adding apple cider vinegar to the broth will help draw out the minerals.

Nutrition researchers Sally Fallon and Kaayla Daniel of the Weston A. Price Foundation explain that **bone broths contain minerals in forms that your body can easily absorb: calcium, magnesium, phosphorus, silicon, sulphur and others.** They contain chondroitin sulphates and glucosamine, to reduce inflammation, arthritis and joint pain.

 I highly recommend you making your own bone broth as the store one uses flavours and MSG.

See my maca powder Main Meals, on how to make your own Chicken broth.

Fabulous foods for the liver – Love Your Liver

Grapefruit
Beetroot
Artichoke
Lemons
(it is alkaline in your body not acidic like you would think)
Turmeric
Avocado
Walnuts
Garlic

Milk thistle is used as a natural treatment for liver problems. These liver problems include cirrhosis, jaundice, hepatitis and gallbladder disorders.

Sprinkle some Spice in your Life

Using more herbs and spices is also a tasty way to boost the nutrition of your diet because.

Turmeric–I love grating this fresh spice into my meals which comes from the same family of spices as ginger. Curcumin is the active ingredient in turmeric, this means both plants can reduce inflammation in arthritis patients . Found in curry powders.

TMH tips Wear gloves as it stains your fingers orange! As I found out.

Oregano–is among the highest in antioxidants of the dried herbs and it goes seamlessly and flavourfully into familiar, everyday foods as well as new recipes.

Cinnamon–While it brings out (and warms up) the flavours in the foods it is paired with, cinnamon will also help keep your arteries healthy, manage blood sugar levels and lower cholesterol. It will help with any sugar cravings.

Cayenne Pepper–Capsicum, the active ingredient in cayenne pepper, has been shown to increase circulation and contribute to weight loss.

Ginger–It may surprise you but one teaspoon of ginger has similar antioxidant levels as one cup of spinach. It can also help with digestive issues (nausea and many others).

Cumin–This spice is an excellent source of minerals like iron, copper, calcium, potassium, manganese, selenium, zinc and magnesium. Cumin seeds contain numerous phyto-chemicals that are known to have antioxidant, carminative and anti-flatulent properties.

Coriander seeds–Unlike other dry spice seeds that lack in vitamin C, coriander seeds contain an ample amount of this anti-oxidant vitamin.

Black pepper–(Piper nigrum)stimulates the taste buds in such a way that an alert is sent to the stomach to increase hydrochloric acid secretion, thereby improving digestion.

Love Your Body

Did you know that the skin is your biggest Organ

So this means that if you really want to have healthy and glowing skin you need to help your liver be super efficient. Your liver has to process all the chemicals that go into our body so, stop layering on toxic moisturisers and creams. They are often loaded with chemicals and toxins, so instead swap your moisturiser for Almond Oil, as it is full of Vitamin A, E and D. It is also great at maintaining a suntan!!

I also only use Natural products around our house. We have fluoride free toothpaste, natural deodorant sticks, and we use essentials oils for our baths (rose oil, tea tree, lavender, epsom bath salts). I use organic skin creams for my face, and we have no nasty air fresheners at home just incense sticks. Just remember that lots of these chemicals weren't here years ago, so all we are doing is going back to a more Natural way of living.

Get Body Brushing!

For many women the dreaded word "Cellulite" installs fear! My little trick to help get rid of this is body Brushing. Cellulite is just a toxic material accumulated in your body's fat cells. Most women tend to store it in our prime sites like under the butt or thighs, so dry skin brushing techniques can really help break down the unwanted toxins!

Relax in a Epsom Sea Salt Bath

As you can probably guess the salts are from Epsom in Surrey. The sulphates in Epsom salt help flush toxins and heavy metals from the cells, which helps ease muscle pain helping the body to eliminate harmful substances. Your skin is a highly porous membrane and adding the right minerals to your bathwater triggers a process called reverse osmosis, which actually pulls salt out of your body, and harmful toxins along with it. For a detoxifying bath, at least once weekly, add two cups of Epsom salts to the water in a bathtub and soak for 10 minutes. Don't go adding in some toxic bubble bath, just keep it natural with salts and natural essential oils.

Makes insulin more effective
Proper magnesium and sulphates levels increase the effectiveness of insulin in the body, helping to lower the risk or severity of diabetes.

We created this delicious blend as we wanted to create a high quality whey protein that people could enjoy without all the artificial sugars and sweeteners. If you are like me and you have a sweet tooth but want to stay in great shape then this is your heaven-sent protein shake!

We only use **Stevia** as a natural sweetener, which is from a plant. It also means it contains zero calories and won't raise your blood sugar levels as other sugars do.

WHY DO WE NEED PROTEIN SHAKES?

First of all Real food always comes first, but these shakes are also ideal as they are so convenient.

First of all what is Protein…? Protein is the building blocks for your muscles, but it also fuels your hormones. Hormones control the time you wake up, your feelings and lots more, so wouldn't it be best to feed these hormones with the nutrients exactly what they need to help you look and feel at your best?

The first 40grams of protein you eat daily supports your immune system, so if you have a low immune system then increase your protein intake. If your hormones are out of balance then you can feel terrible and your diet has a huge influence on them. Alongside Organic eggs, meat and fish **TMH Pure Protein** is a wonderful source of high quality protein.

- **Whey protein shakes can be beneficial for another reason. Our Whey protein can be consumed as a meal or snack. Perfect as a smoothie**

- **They are low in carbohydrates and fat. Our shake can help you feel fuller for longer and help you control your hunger.**

- **Another benefit is the convenience. It takes less than a minute to prepare a protein rich 'meal'.**

- **We also use a TMH Pure Protein as a "natural sweet treat". When you are craving something sweet that is also Nutritious, then we have the ideal snack for you.**

I DON'T EVEN EXERCISE SO I DON'T NEED A PROTEIN SHAKE?

This is even more reason to drink a shake. When it comes to exercising your protein intake should be increased to help the body recover. **TMH Pure Protein** will help you if you are looking to lose weight and build lean muscle for that optimal toned look. It will help your body replenish nutrients for faster results.

However when you aren't exercising you want to help retain the precious muscle that you do have.

*Please note: Not suitable for pets, in fact sweeteners like xylitol and aspartame are poisonous to dogs.

Ed needed a Protein* Fix!

SMOOTHIES AND JUICES

7 DAY TMH KICK START

DAY 1	DAY 2
7.30 – Hot water with fresh lemon	**7.30 –** Hot water with sliced grapefruit
Breakfast Super food eggs	**Breakfast** Apple & cinnamon pie smoothie
	Snack – 10.00 Sliced 2 boiled eggs & pear 20 minutes before lunch – 1 glass of cranberry water
10.15 – Shake **11.00 –** Apple & brazil nuts	
Lunch – 2.00 Zesty tuna salad	**Lunch – 2.00** Left over chicken & chia seed goujons with boosting broccoli salad
5.00 – Snack Juice with spinach, swiss chard, berries, ½ lime, almond milk	**5.00 – Snack** 1 Nectarine & 10 almonds 20 minutes before dinner, 1 glass of cranberry water
7.00 – Dinner Chicken & chia seed goujons (make extra for lunch tomorrow) Side green salad Glass of cranberry water	**7.00 – Dinner** Chicken & spinach curry Make tomorrow's breakfast tonight (bircher muesli – it will only take you 2 mins)

7 DAY TMH KICK START

DAY 3	DAY 4
7.30 – Hot water with fresh lemon	**7.30 –** Hot water with ginger & lemon
Breakfast Bircher muesli (if you didn't make it last night then you can still enjoy it this morning just allow 5 mins to soak)	**Breakfast** Seedy breakfast biscuits ½ pink grapefruit
Shake – 10.15 TMH Protein Shake and some nuts	**Snack – 10.00** Mackerel & beetroot power house
Lunch – 2.00 Left over chicken & spinach curry With kale & spinach leaves salad	**Lunch – 2.00** Baked eggs with ham & tomato (Breakfast section)
Snack – 5.00 Toasted cinnamon pecans	**Snack–5.00** 1 apple sliced and 1 tbsp almond butter
Dinner – 7.00 Lemon, dill & cod caper parcels Make tomorrow's breakfast biscuits	**Dinner – 7.00** Fabulous falafels with balsamic glazed green beans Make a speedy spelt loaf (it will take you 5 minutes tonight and will be so worth it)

7 DAY TMH KICK START

DAY 5

7.30 – Hot water with fresh lemon

Breakfast
Poached eggs, wilted spinach on
2 slices of super spelt loaf

Shake – 10.15
Green & lean smoothie

Lunch – 2.00
Spice rubbed salmon fillet with
spinach & kale salad

Shake – 10.15
Super juice:
Spinach, celery, coconut oil,
green apple, cucumber

Dinner – 7.00
Turkey mince & sweet
potato hash
(make extra for lunch tomorrow)

DAY 6

7.30 – Hot water with fresh lemon

Breakfast
½ pink grapefruit
Choca moca smoothie

Snack – 10.00
Celery and 2 tbsp of almond butter

Lunch – 2.00
Turkey & sweet potato hash

Shake – 10.15
Sesame and almond crackers

Dinner – 7.00
TMH sweet potato cottage pie,
with steamed brocolli and
green beans

7 DAY TMH KICK START

DAY 7

7.30 – Hot water with fresh lemon

Breakfast
Banana & blueberry pancakes

Snack – 10.15
Pear & walnuts

Lunch – 2.00
Grilled lemon roasted chicken pot
with roasted root veg

Shake – 10.15
Sesame & almond crackers

Dinner – 7.00
Moroccan lamb meatballs
with quinoa

Notes...

TMH Fans Getting Inspired in the Kitchen

Scott Ferguson enjoying Gluten free bread

Lynsey McBain recreating TMH Sticky Toffee Pudding

Elouise Coutney recreating TMH Sesame Chicken Goujons

Alexandra Blyth making the Super Speedy Spelt Loaf

Kathryn Potter O'Leary making TMH Almond Crackers for her boys

Amy Andrews making Raspberry & Chocolate TMH Cookies

Maxine Glester making the super Spelt loaf look easy! Looks delicious

Elouise Coutney making her first batch of Gluten free Bagels, tried and tested by John Mahoney who said they were great !

Michelle Scholtka creating TMH Gluten free bread for her family

Julie Bedford is great at recreating TMH recipes to keep her family all Happy and Healthy! Looks Yum !

My Niece Aubrey getting ready to make the Spelt loaf

Hayley Wisken getting creative with TMH Gluten Free Chia bread recipes.

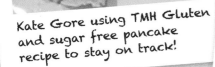

Kate Gore using TMH Gluten and sugar free pancake recipe to stay on track!

Christie Jones & Dan Chamber making TMH Chia seed Goujons all the way in Australia!

Michelle Anderson enjoying TMH Easy Peasy Curry from my first book.

CONTENTS

BREAKFAST

Eat Like A King AND Queen for breakfast!!

Don't Skip Breakfast

The actual meaning of Breakfast, is to "Break" the "fast" of not eating overnight. So if you think about it, your body is busy working hard overnight, helping your body repair physically and mentally, so after all this hard work it will of course need a Nutritious breakfast to start the day.

HERE IS A LITTLE FOOD HISTORY FOR YOU...

The Cereal Story

The idea for corn flakes began by accident when John Harvey Kellogg and his younger brother, Will Keith Kellogg, left some cooked wheat to sit while they got distracted. When they returned, they found that the wheat had gone stale, but being on a strict budget, they decided to continue to process it by forcing it through rollers, hoping to obtain long sheets of the dough. The rest was history, and hey presto Cereals were formed!! A Stale bowl of wheat!

HOW CAN THIS BE NUTRITIOUS?

What your body is actually craving is high quality foods to help it get started and through the busy day ahead. I have lost count the amount of time I have heard "I don't eat breakfast as I am just not hungry in the morning". What I want to point out is that just because you aren't hungry it doesn't mean that your body doesn't need food. It just means that the body had got used to you not giving it any food in the morning and it now has a different routine.

If you really aren't a big breakfast eater then I recommend to start small, few nuts, piece of fruit, a few boiled eggs, or a small smoothie. Try and kick start your hunger in the morning.

The Best Start to my day. A little bit of stretching and relaxing before I get going. ↓

HEALTHY LIFE

My best friends being official taste testers, Claire & Max Doulton, & Emma Jones

This was our view from breakfast the morning after I was proposed to in Barbados.

Think Different

Protein Power Blueberry Biscuits

Prep time: 5 mins
Cooking time: 15 mins
Serves: 3–4

Ingredients

- 150g gluten-free porridge oats
- 2 scoops of TMH vanilla protein powder *(alternatives can be used, just not as nice… I am slightly impartial!)*
- 2 organic eggs
- 1 tbsp honey
- ½ tsp cinnamon
- 100g blueberries
- 250ml almond milk

Method

Preheat the oven to 180°C, and grease a baking sheet with coconut oil.

Blend the oats in a blender until they are a fine crumb. Then in a bowl mix the oat flour, eggs, protein powder, cinnamon, honey and almond milk until all smooth. Lastly add the blueberries and stir.

Scoop the mixture out into cookie size biscuits then bake for 15 minutes.

Truly Madly Healthy
pure protein
Today's Nutrition For Tomorrow's Health

Healthy Homemade Granola Bars

Prep time: 8 mins
Cooking time: 25 mins
Serves: 3–4

Ingredients

- 2 organic bananas mashed in a bowl
- 150g gluten-free oats
- 75g walnuts, chopped
- 75g sunflower seeds
- 75g pumpkin seeds
- 60g ground almonds

TMH tips I have used Banana to sweeten these rather than any extra sugars, and they taste great!

- ¼ cup flax seed *(or whole linseeds)*
  TMH tip: They are the same thing!
- Zest of 1 orange *(optional)*
- 1 tsp cinnamon
- 100ml almond or coconut milk
- 6 tbsp honey
- Pinch of sea salt

Method

Preheat the oven to 180°C then lightly grease a baking tray with parchment paper and coconut oil

Add the oats into a blender and blend until half smooth/half coarse (2–5 seconds). Add the oats into the banana mix and stir.

Crush the walnuts first then add the remaining ingredients into the banana/oat mixture and stir until thoroughly combined.

Spoon the mixture into tray and gently press down until compacted and smooth out with a spoon until even.

Bake for 25 minutes, until firm and lightly golden along the edge. Remove and whilst still warm, cut out the sized bars that you wish to eat. Allow to cool completely then cut and store and enjoy!

TMH tips These can be frozen, just ensure you seal them tightly.

Raw Breakfast Snack Bars

Prep time: 10 mins
Cooking time: 0 *(They are raw)*
Serves: 3–4

Ingredients

- 6 dates, chopped into small pieces
- 50g gluten-free oats
- 6 tbsp raw sunflower seeds
- 6 tbsp crushed almonds *(or ground almonds)*
- 8 tbsp desiccated coconut
- 1–2 tbsp coconut oil *(melted)*
- 2 tbsp chia seeds *(or you can use another seed)*
- 2 tbsp cocoa powder

TMH tips or Cocoa powder is actually heat treated so not technically raw, you can use Cocao Powder which is completely raw.

Method

Place the dates, almonds, desiccated coconut and cocoa into a blender and blend until the mixture is like a thick paste, then add the melted coconut oil, porridge oats, seeds and chia seeds and stir.

Grease and line a large baking dish with greaseproof paper and coconut oil. Place all the mixture in the dish and push down firmly with a wooden spoon or your hand.

Cut your desired shape bars (I like rectangle ones), then place them in the freezer to set for 15 minutes.

Treat Time! For a extra treat, add some dark chocolate chips!! I fancied treating myself whilst I was making this batch!

Chia Seed Pudding

Prep time: 5 mins
Cooking time: 5 mins
Serves: 1

Ingredients

- 8 tbsp chia seeds
- 1 scoop of TMH vanilla protein powder
  TMH tip: just use honey if you don't have this
- 200ml unsweetened almond milk
- 1 tsp cinnamon
- 4 diced strawberries
- 1 tsp honey *(optional if you have a sweet tooth)*

Method

Place the chia seeds into a small pan with the cinnamon and 200ml almond milk, then bring to a simmer over a medium heat.

Continue to stir for 2–5 minutes, until most of the milk has been absorbed and it is a thick consistency.

Remove from the heat, pour into bowl, add a scoop of protein powder and stir well. Add the honey if you are using or don't have protein powder. Add your strawberries on top and serve.

TMH tips Chia Seeds - Packed with Fibre, omega oils and minerals.

38

Chia Seed AND Banana Breakfast Biscuits

Prep time: 5 mins
Cooking time: 15 mins
Serves: 4

Ingredients

- 2 bananas – peeled and mashed
- 50g desiccated coconut
- 3 tbsp chia seeds *(you can use another seed)*
- 150g ground almonds
- 100ml almond or coconut milk
- 1 tbsp raw honey or 1 drop of liquid
- 2 tbsp melted coconut oil

TMH tips Banana contains 20% of your Vitamin B6. Vit B6 is a water-soluble vitamin that plays a role in over 100 different reactions in the body.

Method

Preheat the oven to 180°C and grease and line a baking tray with coconut oil. In a bowl mix the ground almonds, mashed bananas, chia seeds (if using) desiccated coconut and honey. Melt the coconut oil then add this to the bowl. Add the almond milk and roll into ball shapes with your hands. Place them onto the baking try and gently press down, then bake for 15 minutes.

TMH tips Green Veg helps to alkaline the blood and cleanse the system

Enjoy with a nice hot drink!

Seedy Breakfast Biscuits

Prep time: 5 mins
Cooking time: 15 mins
Serves: 4

Ingredients

- 150g gluten-free porridge oats
- 2 organic eggs
- 2 tbsp raw honey
- 100ml coconut or almond milk
- Handful crushed nuts
- 1 tsp cinnamon
- Handful of seeds *(I used sesame)*
- 2 tsp flax seed
- 2 tbsp coconut oil

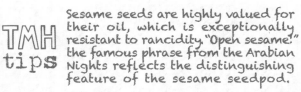

TMH tips

Sesame seeds are highly valued for their oil, which is exceptionally resistant to rancidity. "Open sesame!" the famous phrase from the Arabian Nights reflects the distinguishing feature of the sesame seedpod.

Method

Preheat the oven to 180°C and grease a baking tray with coconut oil. Place the oats into a blender and blitz for 10 seconds, then place them in a large bowl and mix. Add the nuts, seeds, flax seed, cinnamon and stir. In a separate bowl mix the eggs and honey.

Then add the coconut milk and egg mixture to the dry mixture and stir until all the ingredients are combined. Lastly melt the coconut oil and add this to the mixture. Scoop out a tablespoon sized mixture, roll in the seeds again then place onto the baking tray and mould to a biscuit shape or you can set in the freezer for 5 minutes and use a cookie cutter.

Bake for 12–15 minutes.

TMH tips

Raw honey is the most original sweet liquid that honeybees produce from the concentrated nectar of flowers. Collected straight from the extractor; it is totally unheated, unpasteurized, unprocessed honey.

Gluten-free Bagel

Prep time: 10 mins
Cooking time: 15–18 mins
Serves: 2–3

Ingredients

- 2 organic eggs
- 90g tapioca flour
- 60g gluten-free white or brown rice flour
- Pinch of sea salt
- 1 tsp apple cider vinegar
- 1 tsp gluten-free baking powder
- 200ml almond milk
- 1 tsp dry yeast packet
- Optional *(you can make some cinnamon and raisins bagels by adding in 1 tsp of cinnamon and 50g raisins)*

TMH tips Also known as tapioca starch – tapioca helps to add crispness to crusts and gives you that CHEWY texture!

Method

Preheat the oven to 180°C, then grease some ramekins with coconut oil.

In a pan over a medium heat gently warm the almond milk, then add the yeast, stir until it has all dissolved.

Now add both flours, vinegar, sea salt, baking powder and eggs. Stir until smooth and all the flour is combined.

Place the mixture into the greased ramekins and bake in

TMH tips I used a doughnut tray like this for my bagels.

the oven for 15–20 minutes.
Allow to cool, place under the grill.

Speedy Spelt Loaf

Prep time: 2 mins
Cooking time: 20 mins
Serves: 3–4

Ingredients

- 200g organic spelt flour *(avoid if you are a coeliac as contains wheat)*
- 1 tsp gluten-free baking powder
- 6 tbsp greek full fat yoghurt
- Mixed seeds to sprinkle
- Water if needed – 100ml

Method

Preheat the oven to 180°C, and grease a baking tray with coconut oil. In a bowl combine the flour, baking powder and yoghurt. Using your hands make a large ball with the mixture and place on the baking tray. Score the bread in 4 then sprinkle with seeds.

Bake for 20 minutes, allow to cool then enjoy! It reminds me of sour dough bread, nice and rustic.

TMH tips

The gluten in spelt flour is a little unusual. Unlike wheat flour, which is quite resilient and often needs a long kneading time (with breads) to strengthen its gluten and give the bread structure, the gluten in spelt flour breaks down fairly easily.

Great for a Sunday Morning lay-in!

Avocado on Spelt Toast

Using the Speedy Spelt bread recipe on the page before. Slice the loaf and place under a grill for a few moments, then add fresh sliced avocado on top.

2 slices of spelt bread

- 1 avocado
- Black pepper

This combination is still one of my absolute favourites!

Healthy Chocolate Spread on Toast or why not add a spoonful to your Porridge!

GOOD MORNING SUNDAY

HEAVEN IN A BOWL!!

Smoked Salmon ~and~ Avocado on Toast

Prep time: 2 mins

Cooking time: 0 *(as the bread is already baked)*

Serves: 1

Ingredients

- 2 slices of spelt bread *(recipe on previous page)*
- ½ avocado sliced
- 2 slices organic smoked salmon
- Juice ¼ lemon

Method

Layer the avocado on to the bread, then add the smoked salmon, then sprinkle some black pepper and the juice of ¼ lemon.

Homemade Chocolate Spread

Prep time: 5 mins

Cooking Time: 0 *(if you are already using one of my bread recipes)*

Ingredients

- 4 tbsp hazelnut butter
- 1 tbsp cocoa powder
- 30ml almond milk
- 1 tsp honey

Method

To make the Chocolate Spread – In a bowl mix the hazelnut butter, almond milk, honey, cocoa powder and stir until smooth, you can adjust this to your liking by adding in either more cocoa or honey.

Glorious Gluten-free Toast

Prep time: 5 mins
Cooking time: 30 mins
Serves: 4–5

Ingredients

- 180g ground almonds
- 80g arrowroot
  TMH tip: This is a gluten-free thickener ideal for cakes and bread
- 3 tbsp ground flaxseed
- 1 tbsp gluten-free baking powder *(no need for yeast)*
- 3 organic eggs
- 1 tbsp coconut oil
- 1 tbsp honey *(optional)*
- Pinch of sea salt
- 3 tbsp sesame seeds *(optional)*

Method

Preheat the oven to 180°C and grease the tin and grease a loaf tin liner. In a large bowl mix the almonds, arrowroot, flaxseed, baking powder and salt. Then in a separate bowl whisk the eggs until light and fluffy, add the honey to the egg mixture. Pour the egg mixture into the dry mix and fold, lastly melt the coconut oil and add to the bowl. Pour the mixture into the loaf tin, sprinkle the seeds on top and bake for 30 minutes, or until your knife comes out clean.

Allow to cool, turn out and enjoy. This bread is even better when it is toasted!!

TMH tips
Perfect with Organic Grass Feed Butter or Almond Nut Butter. I have made lots of variations, Rosemary and Sunflower Seed, Chia Seed & Honey. Just add your favourite ingredients.

Better than Sliced Bread

Prep time: 10 mins
Cooking time: 40 mins
Serves: 4–5

Ingredients

- 250g dovecote farm gluten-free flour
- 3 eggs
- 2 tsp baking powder
- 250ml almond milk *(or another dairy free milk)*
- 1 tbsp coconut oil melted
- Pinch of salt
- Diced fresh rosemary *(optional)*
- 4 tbsp sunflower and chia seeds

Method

Preheat the oven to 180° and grease and line a bread tin with baking paper and coconut oil (or butter).

In a large bowl combine the flour, salt and baking powder.

In another bowl mix the almond milk, eggs, rosemary and 3 tablespoons of seeds. Lastly melt the coconut oil and add this to the milk mixture.

Fold the two bowls together and pour the mixture into the bread tin. Sprinkle the remaining seeds on top and bake for 40 minutes.

Allow to cool, place under the grill and toast!

This bread was so popular I made 40 loaves in one night to sell at Excel Gym. Best thing since gluten-free sliced bread !

Banana AND Blueberry Pancakes – a Kids Favourite

Prep time: 5 mins
Cooking time: 5 mins
Serves: 2

Ingredients

- 2 bananas mashed
- 100g blueberries
- 1 tbsp coconut oil
- 1 tsp cinnamon
- 100g gluten-free porridge oats
- 200ml almond milk
- 2 organic eggs

TMH tips You don't need any extra sugar as the natural sugar in the banana is sweet enough.

Method

Blend the porridge oats into a flour consistency in a blender for 10 seconds.

In a bowl mash the banana with a fork, add the eggs and cinnamon. Add the oats, blueberries and almond milk and mix thoroughly. Heat the coconut oil in a pan over a medium heat, add a spoonful of the pancake mix into the pan. Allow to cook for approx. 1 minute then flip over.

Serve with your favourite toppings, seeds, berries, honey.

Raspberry Pancakes with Whipped Coconut Cream

Prep time: 5 mins

Cooking time: 10 mins

Serves: 2

Ingredients

- 2 egg whites
- 40g coconut flour – sieved
- 150ml almond milk
- 1 tsp vanilla essence
- ½ tsp gluten-free baking powder
- Pinch of sea salt
- ½ tsp cinnamon
- Stevia *(I use either 1 drop or you can use 1 tbsp honey)*
- 2 tbsp coconut cream
- 1 tsp honey
- Fresh raspberries & blueberries for the topping

Method

Combine the egg whites, coconut flour, milk, vanilla, gluten-free baking powder, cinnamon and salt into a bowl and stir. Heat a pan and melt the coconut oil over medium heat until the pan is hot. Pour your desired amount of batter into the pan and cook until golden, a few minutes on each side. Re-grease the pan with coconut oil and do the same with the remaining mix.

To make the Cream, pour the cream into a bowl, add the honey and whisk until it starts to thicken, then smother on top of your pancakes, layer them with cream and the fresh berries.

BREAKFAST POWER POTS

YOUR
HEALTH
IS
YOUR
WEALTH

STAY RICH WITH OUR NUTRITION AND FITNESS PR

Avocado and Apple Porridge

Prep time: 5 mins
Cooking time: 5 mins
Serves: 2

Ingredients

- ½ avocado *(per person)*
- 1 small apple, diced and peeled
- 100g gluten-free oats
- 200ml almond milk
- 1 scoop of TMH protein *(if you don't have this you can use 1 tsp honey)*
- Handful of red grapes

Method

Peel and dice the apple into small pieces.

Place the oats, diced apple and almond milk into a pan and simmer for 3–5 minutes. In the meantime, dice the avocado and once the porridge oats are cooked, pour into a bowl, add the protein or honey and stir well.

Add the avocado and grapes on top.

Enjoy this creamy combination.

THE NIGHT BEFORE BREAKFAST POTS

Trust Me! This is Delicious!!

Bircher Muesli

Prep time: 5 mins
Cooking time: 0 mins
Serves: 1

Ingredients

- 40g gluten-free oats *(per person)*
- 150ml almond milk
- Fresh berries
- 1 tsp honey
- 1 scoop of TMH protein powder *(optional)*
- Seeds

Method

Place the oats in the bottom of an airtight jar, add the milk and stir. If you are adding the protein powder do so now and place in the fridge overnight.

In the morning top with the fresh fruit, honey and seeds and enjoy. I also like some extra crunch from some seeds.

This takes 2 minutes the night before and you can just grab it and go in the morning!

Overnight Almond AND Buckwheat Porridge

Prep time:
Overnight soaking
Cooking Time: 0
Serves: 1

Ingredients

- 90g buckwheat groats
- 1 tbsp honey
- 1 banana
- 75g almonds
- 150ml almond milk

Method

Soak the buckwheat groats in water overnight in the fridge. In the morning, wash them as they will be slimey, which is normal.

Place half into a blender with the banana, honey and almonds and blend. Now pour into a bowl, add the remaining buckwheat groats, top with almond milk and stir!

This can be stored for 2–3 days!

Here are what buckwheat groats look like !

Power Protein Porridge

Prep time: 5 mins
Cooking time: 3–5 mins
Serves: 1

Ingredients

- 50g gluten-free porridge oats *(per person)*
- 1 scoop TMH pure protein
- 2 tbsp chia seeds *(optional)*
- 200ml almond milk
- 60g fresh berries
- Seeds to sprinkle

Method

Place the porridge oats, chia seeds and almond milk in a pan and heat for 3–5 minutes. Stirring occasionally. Once all the water is absorbed, place into a bowl and add the scoop of protein. Stir well until all combined, then sprinkle with your fruit and seeds.

TMH tips Power your Saturdays with Protein Porridge!

Sit back, relax and enjoy your meal!

«— HELLO —»
WEEKEND

Goodness Goddess Granola

Prep time: 5 mins
Cooking time: 15–18 mins
Serves: 3

Ingredients

- 300g gluten-free oats
- 50g desicated coconut
- 150g nuts *(I use almonds, hazelnuts and walnuts)*
- 2 tbsp coconut oil
- 3 tbsp honey
- 150g dried cranberries *(optional)*

Method

Preheat the oven to 180°C then add the coconut oil in a roasting tray and place it in the oven to melt for 2 minutes. Remove the tray from the oven then add the honey and stir with coconut oil, now add the porridge oats, desiccated coconut, nuts and dried fruit. TMH tip: Add some cocoa powder for a chocolate flavour. Coat them all evenly and place back in the oven for 8 minutes, stir halfway then again for another 8 minutes.

 TMH tips Make a big batch for the week and store it!

Toasted Nuts to Go

Prep time: 30 mins
Cooking time: 5 mins
Serves: 2–3

Ingredients

- 25g cashew
- 25g almonds
- 25g pecans
- 25g sesame seeds
- 25g pumpkin seeds
- 1 tsp of cinnamon
- 3 dates – diced
- 1 tsp sea salt
- Dried fruit *(optional)*
- 25g desiccated coconut

Method

In a bowl of water, add the sea salt and soak the nuts for at least 30 minutes. Drain and pat dry, in a pan melt the coconut oil, diced dates and cinnamon for 1 minute until the dates become soft. Then add the nuts and seeds and fry for 4 minutes, keep stirring to toast them all evenly. Serve then sprinkle the desiccated coconut over them for a crunchy texture.

Enjoy with a bowl of almond milk or full fat greek yoghurt .

Chia Seed AND Almond Butter Bites

Prep time : 15 mins
Cooking time : 18 mins
Serves: 3–4

Ingredients

- 100g gluten-free flour *(blended to a flour)*
- 2 tbsp cocoa or cacao powder
- 2 tbsp almond butter
- 3 tbsp seeds *(any)*
- 1 banana mashed
- 4 tbsp chia seeds *(soaked in 100ml almond milk for at least 10 minutes)*

 TMH tips Cocoa powder also contains phosphorus, magnesium and calcium, which build bones, tissues and nerves in the body.

Method

Soak the chia seeds in the almond milk for at least 10 minutes.

Preheat the oven to 180°C and grease a baking tray.

In a bowl mash the banana, then add the ground oats, almond butter, cococa powder seeds and the chia seed mix.

Scoop on to the baking tray and bake for 10–12 minutes. I cut mine into mini shapes once cooled.

SMOOTHIES AND JUICES

Smoothies

Smoothies are great for a busy morning as you can blend and be out the door in minutes. The main thing to remember with smoothies is that you don't just have loads of fruit and water. To make them into more of a complete meal then they need to contain, protein, fats and carbohydrates.

Ed and I Blackberry picking for our Smoothies!

Here is a little checklist to help you build the best smoothie:

Protein - TMH Pure Protein Powder • Vegan Protein Powder • Nuts • Seeds and Nut Butter

Carbohydrates - All Fruit • All Vegetables • Porridge Oats Luccuma Powder

Fats - Almond Milk • Nuts • Seeds • Nut Butter • Coconut Milk • Avocado and Oil

Spices - Cinnamon • Nutmeg • Ginger • Fresh Mint Cocoa or Cocao Powder

Liquids - Water • Fresh Lemons and Lime Juice Cranberry Juice • Almond Milk • Coconut Milk • Ice Hazelnut Milk

Before we get started on all the smoothies and juices, you will notice that I recommend Almond Milk, which you can buy unsweetened ones in the long life milk section. However if you want to make your own, then here is my recipe...

Almond Milk

Prep time: Min 2 hours
Cooking time: 0
Serves: 3–4

Ingredients

- 500g almonds
- 500ml water
- 1f you want a sweetened version add 1 tsp honey

Method

Soak the almonds in water for a minimum of 2 hours, the longer you soak them the more creamier they will be (I like to do mine for approx. 2 days) Once soaked, strain them and run them under cold water to rinse them thoroughly.

Then place them into a blender with 2 cups of water and blend for 2 minutes, next line a sieve with either a cheese cloth or muslin over a bowl and empty the mix in to the cloth. Allow the mix to strain then gather the cloth and squeeze out the excess milk. You will get approx. 3–4 cups worth, store in a fridge and use within 2–3 days.

If you wish to add sweetness, then add honey.

Chia AND Almond Chocolate Delight

Prep time: 2 mins
Cooking time: 0 mins
Serves: 1

Ingredients

- 1 tbsp almond butter
- 200ml almond milk
- 5 tbsp chia seeds
- ½ banana TMH Tip – Wrap the other half in cling film and freeze for next time
- 1 tbsp cocoa powder
- ¼ tsp cinnamon TMH Tip – For a protein hit, add 1 scoop of TMH pure protein

TMH tips I have a tsp of Nut butter in the afternoon as a little energy booster!

Method

In a blender mix everything together until like a pudding consistency. If you want it sweeter then add a drizzle of raw honey or sprinkle some fresh fruit.

After Eight Chocolate Delight

Prep time: 5 mins
Cooking time: 0 mins
Serves: 2

Ingredients

- 1 tbsp cocoa powder
- 6 fresh mint leaves TMH Tip – Did you know the menthol oil derived from mint can be very soothing for nausea and related motion sickness.
- ¼ (avocado) for some extra creaminess
- 1 date
- 1 small banana
- 1 scoop of TMH vanilla protein
- 200ml almond milk

Method

Blend until smooth, sit back and relax.

This recipe is inspired by my love of all things Chocolate and Mint!

Choca Moca

Prep time: 1 min
Cooking time: 0 mins
Serves: 1

Ingredients

- 1 tbsp almond butter
- 250ml almond milk
- 1 tsp cocoa powder
- ½ banana *(ideally frozen)*
- 1 scoop TMH vanilla pure protein powder
- ½ tsp honey
- Dash of cinnamon

Method

Place all the ingredients into a blender and blitz, sprinkle with cinnamon.

This is a Smoothie from my TMH Smoothie Bar

TMH tips

Little Max enjoying a tasty TMH Smoothie

Get Up AND Go Go Espresso

Prep time: 2 mins
Cooking time: 0 mins
Serves: 1

This is so popular that it is served in a local coffee bar in Leigh-on-Sea!

Ingredients

- 1 organic espresso shot
- 1 scoop of TMH vanilla pure protein powder TMH Tip: One scoop contains a whopping 27g of protein
- 1 tsp coconut oil
- 100ml almond or coconut milk hot or cold

Method

Place all the ingredients into a blender and blend for 15 seconds.

TMH tips Always go for Organic Coffee as they contain far less mould and pesticides than conventional coffee.

TMH tips Bulletproof is a brand I use as Cheaper coffee varieties cost less because they use poor quality beans and they allow a higher percentage of damaged (mouldy) beans, then companies process them with techniques that add flavour but amplify the amount of toxins.

GIVEN ENOUGH
COFFEE
I COULD RULE THE
WORLD

Apple Cinnamon Pie

Prep time: 1 min
Cooking time: 0 mins
Serves: 1

Ingredients

- 1 organic apple chopped and peeled
- 1 scoop TMH pure vanilla protein powder
- 1 tsp cinnamon
- ½ tsp vanilla essence *(optional)*
- Handful of almonds or 1 tsp almond butter
- 200ml coconut or almond milk

Method

Blend all the ingredients in a blender until smooth, sprinkle some extra cinnamon on top.

Green AND Lean Smoothie

Prep time: 5 mins
Cooking time: 0 mins
Serves: 2

Ingredients

- 2 organic apples
- 1 organic orange
- 2 handfuls of spinach
- 2 handfuls of kale
- 1 avocado
- 400ml water
- Handful of fresh mint
- Juice of 1 lime

Method

Dice and peel the apples and orange first then, blend all the ingredients until smooth.

Banana-rama

Prep time: 2 mins
Cooking time: 0 mins
Serves: 2

Ingredients

- 60g gluten-free oats
- 1 banana
- 2 scoops of TMH vanilla protein powder
- 500ml coconut or almond milk
- 1 tsp cinnamon

Method

Place all the ingredients into a blender for 15 seconds until smooth (note it will remain quite thick because of the oats).

Fuel for Busy Days!

Banana

Green Tea Dream

Prep time: 1 min
Cooking time: 0 mins
Serves: 1

Ingredients

- 20g gluten-free oats
- 2 tsp flax seed
- 1 scoop of TMH pure protein powder
- 300ml almond milk
- ¼ tsp matcha green tea powder
- ½ banana
- 3 ice cubes

Method

Blend all the ingredients into
a blender and enjoy.

TMH tips I use Matcha green tea powder. →

Superfood Superhuman Smoothie

Prep time: 3 mins
Cooking time: 0 mins
Serves: 2

Ingredients

- 1 avocado
- 1 tbsp chia seeds
- 1 tsp coconut oil
- 1 banana
- 1 scoop of TMH vanilla pure protein
- ½ tsp macha green tea
- ½ tsp cocoa powder
- 5 ice cubes
- 350ml almond milk

Method

Blend and enjoy your energized day ahead.

After drinking this smoothie it makes you feel like you can take on the world !

GOOD MORNING beautiful WORLD

Chia Berry Booster

Prep time: 3 mins
Cooking time: 0 mins
Serves: 2

Ingredients

- 500ml almond milk
- 4 tbsp chia seeds
- 200g frozen berries
- 2 scoops of TMH pure protein powder

Method

Blend everything together in a blender until smooth (the chia seeds will make the consistency quite thick) so don't expect it to be really smooth.

BERRIES

Flu Fighting

Prep time: 3 mins
Cooking time: 0 mins
Serves: 2

Ingredients

- 2 handfuls of spinach
- 2 handfuls of kale
- 1 orange TMH Tip – Vitamin C
- 1 handful of fresh mint
- 1 tbsp almond butter
- 1 scoop of greens powder (optional – chlorella, wheatgrass)
- 1 avocado
- 300ml water
- 4 ice cubes

Method

Blend and enjoy this immune boosting drink.

Breakfast Shot?! This was a Pre-run Green Shot full of wheatgrass, spinach, chlorella and aloe vera juice.

TMH tips

Oranges are full of beta-carotene which is a powerful antioxidant which protects the skin from free radicals and prevents the signs of ageing.

Just Beet It!

Prep time: 2 mins
Cooking time: 0 mins
Serves: 1

Ingredients

- 1 cooked beetroot
- 100g frozen raspberries
- 1 tbsp honey
- 200ml almond milk

Method

Blend all together and enjoy.

Notes...

PACKED WITH PROTEIN

TRULY
HEAL

LUNCH
'N'
DINNER

WHICH FIRST THE
CAME Chicke
OR THE Egg
?

Super Food Eggs

Prep time: 2 mins
Cooking time: 6 mins
Serves: 2

Ingredients

- 4 organic eggs
- 4 handfuls spinach
- 1 avocado sliced *(½ each)*
- 1 tsp balsamic vinegar
- 2 tbsp seeds

Method

Place the eggs into a pan of cold water, and boil for at least 4 minutes. In a bowl add the raw spinach leaves, slice the avocado on top, then once the eggs have boiled and cooled, shell them, layer on top drizzle with the balsamic vinegar and seeds.

This is a great snack for my train journeys to London! Maybe not for the other passengers

Free Range

Mackerel, Seeds AND Beetroot Power House

Prep time: 2 mins
Cooking time: 0 mins
Serves: 2

Ingredients

- 2 cooked beetroots – sliced
- 2 mackerel fillets – smoked
- 4 handfuls of kale
- 2 inches cucumbe – diced
- ½ tsp coconut oil
- 1 tsp ground cumin
- 1 tbsp dill – diced

· Method

In a pan heat the coconut oil over a medium heat, then add the cumin and cook for minute, then add the kale and fry for a further minute. Finally add the beetroot to the pan for 30 seconds and pour into a bowl. Mix the cucumber and dill into the bowl and serve alongside the mackerel fillets.

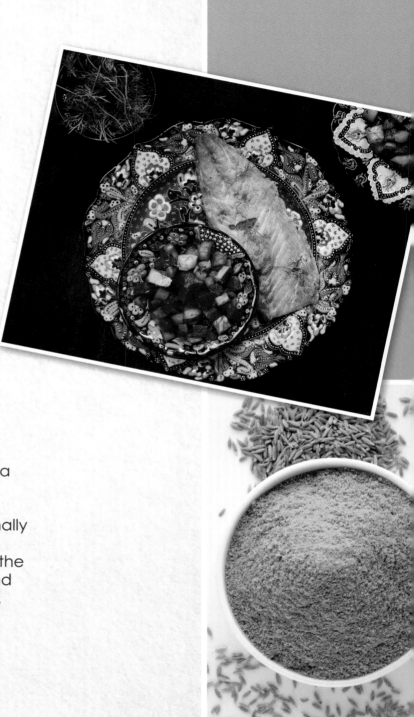

Baked Eggs with Ham & Tomato

Prep time: 5 mins
Cooking time: 12–14 mins
Serves: 2

Ingredients

- 1 garlic clove, chopped
- A few basil leaves – shredded
- 4 large plum tomatoes
- 4 slices cooked ham, roughly torn
- 4 organic eggs

TMH tips The yolk is loaded with nutrients, like bioflavonoids, brain fats like phosphatidyl choline, powerful antioxidants and sulphur.

Method

Heat the oven to 180°C, then heat a little oil in a pan, sizzle the garlic for a few seconds then scoop out the inside of the tomatoes and add those to the pan and simmer all of these for 5 minutes until thickened.

Stir in the basil, then divide the sauce and shredded ham between the now empty plum tomatoes. Crack an egg in the middle and Bake for 12–14 minutes until just set.

Turkey Scotch Egg

Prep time: 10 mins
Cooking time: 15 mins
Serves: 2

Ingredients

- 5 organic eggs (1 egg is for extra one for coating the balls)
- 300g turkey mince
- 1 tbsp rosemary – diced
- Sea salt and black pepper
- 150g desiccated coconut

Method

Preheat oven to 180°C.

Bring a pan of water to boil then add 4 eggs, reduce the heat to simmer then boil them for 6 minutes. In a bowl mix the turkey meat, rosemary, and season.

Divide the mixture into 4 even balls, then flatten them out on a chopping board approx. 12 x 7 cm. Take the eggs and place one in the middle of the meat, then gently wrap the meat around the egg until it is all sealed.

Then place the one remaining raw egg in a bowl and whisk, gently roll the balls in the egg then dip them straight into the desiccated coconut.

These are perfect to take on a Picnic!

TMH tips
Drain and cool the eggs and place them under running water, then peel. (it makes them so much easier to peel)

In a pan melt 3 tablespoons of coconut oil over a medium heat, add the balls and cook until they start to turn golden, transfer to the oven and bake for 20 mins. Coconut oil is quite expensive so rather than having to use huge amounts of oil to fry them in, it is best to just shallow fry them and pop them in the oven after.

Salmon and Egg Muffins

Prep time: 5 mins
Cooking time: 18–20 mins
Serves: 2–3

Ingredients

- 3 organic eggs
- Precooked salmon fillet – flaked
- 2 spring onions – diced
- 1 tomato – diced
- ½ red pepper

Method

Preheat the oven to 180°C, then you can either grease a muffin tray with coconut oil or I usually put them in muffin cases as they are easy to grab on the go and kids like the idea of a muffin. Dice the spring onions, tomato and pepper. Whisk the eggs then add the tomato and flaked salmon to the mix. Evenly pour into tray and bake for 18–20 minutes.

Vegetable Frittata

Prep time: 5 mins
Cooking time: 0 mins
Serves: 4

Ingredients

- 2 courgettes – sliced
- 1 red pepper – sliced
- 150g baby spinach
- 8 eggs
- 1 onion – diced
- 1 tbsp coconut oil
- Fresh basil leaves

Method

In a pan heat the coconut oil then add the onion and cook for a few minutes. Then add the courgettes and cook for another 3–5 minutes. Add the spinach and let it wilt down. In a small bowl lightly beat the eggs, season and add the fresh basil. Pour the egg into the pan with the vegetables and distribute evenly.

Cook over a low heat until the base is set but still some liquid on top. Heat the grill and place the frittata under to cook the top for 2–3 minutes.

Season and serve.

TMH tips Great for all the family to enjoy together.

Notes...

LUNCH & DINNER

Poultry

Geese

Chickens

Quail

Turkeys

Ducks

BBQ

iN broccoli WE trust

Natural is better

100%

Farm ORGANIC Fresh

Products

Chicken Shaslik AND Onion Bhajis – Great for a Midweek Meal

Prep time: 5 mins
Cooking time: 20 mins
Serves: 2

Ingredients

- 2 red peppers – diced
- 2 chicken breasts – diced
- 2 plum tomoatos – diced
- 1 onion – diced
- 3 tbsp madras curry powder
- 1 tbsp coconut oil
- Handful coriander

Method

Dice the chicken breasts and coat with olive oil and 1 tablespoon of madras curry powder and allow it to marinate. Heat a skillet over a medium pan and add the remaining 2 tablespoons of madras powder, fry for 1 minute then add the diced chicken to the pan. Allow the chicken to brown then add the onion, pepper and tomato and coat in the curry powder. Keep turning over to cook evenly for approx. 12–15 minutes and serve. Lastly sprinkle with freshly diced coriander.

Onion Bahjis

Prep time: 10 mins
Cooking time: 5 mins
Serves: 2

Ingredients

- 2 white onions – halved then sliced
- 2 eggs
- 1 tsp turmeric
- 1 tsp ground coriander
- 1½ tbsp coconut flour
- 1 tbsp coconut oil

Method

Place the eggs into a bowl and hand whisk for a few minutes, then add all the ingredients to the bowl, mix well and season. Make sure that all the onions are coated and then roll them into ball shapes.

Melt the coconut oil in a shallow pan over a medium heat and drop the balls into the oil. Fry on each side for 1 minute, then turn over. Repeat the process for the remaining mixture and add more oil if needed.

Serve with a squeeze of fresh lemon juice.

Thai Spiced Turkey Stir Fry

Prep time: 10 mins
Cooking time: 15 mins
Serves: 2

Ingredients

- 2 organic turkey steaks – diced into small pieces
- 1 lime
- 1 red chilli – diced
- ½ inch fresh ginger
- 1 red onion – diced
- 2 garlic cloves – sliced thinly
- 4 handfuls spinach
- 2 handfuls kale
- 1 tsp coconut oil
- 1 tsp five spice
- Holy basil leaves *(optional)*

Also known as "Tulsi" or "The Incomparable One," holy basil is one of the most sacred plants in India. Holy basil has been used to treat a variety of conditions – everything from the common cold to bronchitis to fever to certain digestive complaints, including ulcers

Method

In a skillet heat 1 teaspoon of coconut oil over a medium heat then add the chilli, ginger, onion, garlic and five spice and fry for a few minutes. Add the turkey meat and fry for a few minutes on each side, lastly add the spinach, kale and basil leaves and cook for 1 minute. Squeeze the lime juice over the top and serve with fresh coriander.

Crunchy Coconut AND Chia Seed Chicken Goujons

TMH tips These are one of my favorite recipes in this book.

Prep time: 10 mins
Cooking time: 12–15 mins
Serves: 2–3

Ingredients

- 200g desiccated coconut
- 2 organic chicken breasts – diced
- 2 organic eggs
- 50g chia seeds *(optional)*
- 1 tsp coconut oil
- 4 tbsp curry powder

Method

Preheat the oven to 180°C and grease and line a baking tray with coconut oil. Get three separate bowls and place the curry powder into one of them, hand whisk the eggs in another, then add the desiccated coconut and chia seeds in the third bowl. Firstly roll the chicken in the curry powder, then dip the chicken into the egg bowl, lastly roll the chicken into the coconut and chia seed mix. Place on the baking tray and roast for 25 minutes, and turn them halfway.

Garlic Avocado Dip

Prep time: 5 mins
Cooking time: 0! Woo-hoo
Serves: 2

Ingredients

- 1 avocado
- Juice ½ orange
- 1 garlic clove *(optional)*
- 100ml coconut/almond milk or water
- Seasoning

Method

Place all the ingredients into a blender and blend until a smooth creamy texture.

 TMH tips These are a match made in Heaven; you can just dunk your Goujons into the dip!

Herby Healthy Chicken Kebabs

TMH tips You can marinate the day before if you are that prepared as it makes them even more moist

Prep time: 10 mins
Cooking time: 20 mins
Serves: 2

Ingredients

- 2 organic chicken breasts
- 3 tbsp greek/bio yoghurt
- 2 tbsp curry powder
- Handful fresh basil – diced
- 1 red and 1 yellow pepper – diced
- 1 onion – diced
- 2 garlic cloves – sliced thinly
- 4 handfuls spinach
- 2 handfuls kale
- 1 tbsp coconut oil
- 1 tsp five spice
- Holy basil leaves *(optional)*

 TMH tips To stop the sticks from burning, soak them in water for a minute

TMH tips Why not try my Garlic Pesto in the sides and dips section on another day.

Method

Dice the chicken into inch-sized pieces, and then in a bowl mix the yoghurt, curry powder and basil until all combined. Allow to marinate for at least 30 minutes in the fridge. Heat 1 tablespoon of coconut oil in a griddle and make your kebabs with kebab sticks. Place on the griddle and fry for 4 minutes on each side until cooked through.

These are great on top of a leafy green salad or roasted vegetables.

Chilli *and* Lime Marinated Chicken

Prep time: 5 mins
Cooking time: 15 mins
Serves: 2

Ingredients

For the marinade

- 6 tbsp organic olive oil
- 1 tsp honey
- 1 red chilli – diced thinly
- Juice from 1 lime

Seasoning

- 1 tbsp coconut oil
- 2 chicken breasts – diced
- 4 tomatoes – diced
- 1 white onion – diced
- ¼ cucumber – diced

Method

Blend all the marinade ingredients together then place them in a sandwich bag, add the chicken breast, massage the marinade into them evenly then allow to marinate for at least 30 minutes.

Once ready, heat 1 tablespoon of coconut oil in a griddle pan over a medium heat and grill on each side for at least 4–5 minutes, Keep turning until cooked thoroughly then serve.

I served ours with the diced tomato, onion and cucumber diced salsa.

Super Sprouting Chicken Salad

Prep time: 5 mins
Cooking time: 15 mins
Serves: 2

Ingredients

- Alfalfa sprouts *(you can get these in the salad section of the supermarkets)*
- 2 organic chicken breasts – diced
- Handful thyme – diced
- 4 handfuls spinach
- 2 handfuls kale
- 8 cherry tomatoes – diced
- 3 tbsp olive oil
- 3 tbsp balsamic vinegar
- 1 tsp coconut oil

TMH tips

Alfalfa sprouts are the shoots of the alfalfa plant, harvested before they become the full-grown plant. Because they are so small, the sprouts contain a concentrated amount of certain vitamins and minerals such as calcium, vitamin K and vitamin C.

Method

Marinate the chicken in 1 tablespoon of olive oil and the diced thyme. Heat the coconut oil in a griddle pan over a medium heat and once melted add the chicken breasts and grill on each side for at least 5–6 minutes.

In a large salad bowl mix the spinach, kale, cherry tomatoes and mix. In a small dish mix the olive oil and balsamic vinegar, season then dress the salad.

Finally once the chicken is cooked, add to the salad, sprinkle the sprouts on top and enjoy.

Turkey Mince AND Sweet Potato Hash

Prep time: 10 mins
Cooking time: 15 mins
Serves: 2–3

Ingredients

- 2 small to medium sweet potatoes – peeled and diced
- 1 apple – peeled cored and diced
- 2 tbsp coconut oil, divided
- ¼ tsp cinnamon *(optional)*
- 3 spring onions – diced
- 400g turkey mince
- 3 large handfuls baby spinach
- 1 white onion – diced

TMH tips

If you suffer from poor digestion or tummy bloating try adding coconut oil to your diet. Coconut oil has been found to benefit digestive disorders including irritable bowel syndrome and microbial related tummy bugs.

Method

In a large pan heat 1 tablespoon coconut oil over medium-high heat. Once heated, add diced sweet potatoes and apples. Add a pinch or two of sea salt and cinnamon to the pan. Cook sweet potatoes and apples until cooked and softened. I prefer my sweet potatoes to be slightly browned.

While the sweet potatoes are cooking, heat a large pan with 1 tablespoon coconut oil over medium heat. Add the turkey mince and onion to the pan, then add the spinach and wilt down. Once spinach is cooked add the sweet potato apple mixture to pan and stir to combine all. Lastly add the diced spring onion, stir and serve.

This is a nice mix of sweet and savoury.

Moroccan Lamb Meatballs

Prep time: 30 mins
Cooking time: 35 mins
Serves: 4

Ingredients

- 500g organic lamb mince
- 50g gluten-free oats *(blended to a flour)* or an alternative gluten-free flour
- 1 egg beaten
- 1 handful fresh mint
- 1 tbsp harissa paste
- 2 tsp ground cumin
- 2 tsp ground coriander
- 1 tbsp coconut oil

Our visit to the spice markets in Morocco.

Method

In a bowl mix the lamb mince, 1 egg, mint, cumin, harrisa and coriander and stir well.

Roll them into approx. 14–16 small balls and set in the fridge for 30 minutes.

Heat the coconut oil in a pan over a medium heat, fry the balls on each side for 5–6 minutes and transfer to the oven to keep warm.

Make the Quinoa Salad

Place the quinoa in water and simmer for desired cooking time (usually 6–10 minutes). Drain, rinse then add to a bowl. Dress the quinoa, fresh mint, seeds and the olive oil. Now serve with the lamb meatballs on top.

The Perfect Homemade Beef Burgers

Prep time: 30 mins
Cooking time: 10 mins
Serves: 2–3

Ingredients

- 500g organic mince
- 1 tsp dijon mustard
- Sea salt and black pepper
- A few sprigs of fresh rosemary – diced
- 1 tsp coconut oil

Method

In a large bowl combine the mince, mustard, rosemary and season. Using your hand make approx. 6–8 burgers and heat a griddle pan. Add the coconut oil and grill on each side for 5–8 minutes.

TMH tips
If you put the patties in the fridge it will help them stay together.

TMH tips
Try My Garlic Avocado Dip as a burger topping and you dont need a burger bun why not try some grilled portabella mushrooms!!

Chicken Buckwheat Noodle Stir Fry

Prep time: 15 min
Cooking time: 20 mins
Serves: 2

Ingredients

- 100g each of either buckwheat or soba noodles
- 2 chicken breasts – diced into very small pieces
- 2 garlic cloves crushed
- ½ inch ginger
- 1 onion – sliced

- 2 tbsp apple cider vinegar
- 1 red pepper – diced
- 1 tbsp turmeric
- 2 chillis – diced
- 1 tbsp coconut oil
- 1 handful holy basil leaves
- Sesame seeds to garnish

Method

Boil the noodles in a pan of water for approx. 3 minutes until soft, drain. Drizzle with olive oil and set aside.

In a frying pan, fry the coconut oil, chilli, ginger, onion and turmeric until soft. Then add the chicken breasts, apple cider vinegar and peppers and cook thoroughly on each

side (approx. 3 minutes a side)

Add the basil leaves and the noodles and coat well.

Chicken AND Spinach Curry

Prep time: 15 min
Cooking time: 20 mins
Serves: 2

Ingredients

For the paste

- 1 tbsp garam masala
- 1 tbsp turmeric
- 1 tbsp ground coriander
- 1 tbsp paprika
- 1 red chilli – diced
- 2 tbsp olive oil
- Juice ½ lemon
- Bunch of coriander – diced
- Chicken breast – diced
- 1 onion – sliced
- Fresh spinach leaves *(5 handfuls)*
- 150ml coconut or almond milk

 TMH tips Swap the chicken to chickpeas for a vegetarian option.

Method

In a pestle and mortar combine all the paste ingredients until they come to a paste.

Heat 1 teaspoon of coconut oil in a pan, then add the onion and gently fry for a few minutes.

Scoop the curry paste into the pan and fry for 30 seconds, now add the chicken and coat well.

Cook the chicken for 3–4 minutes on each side until thoroughly cooked, now add the coconut or almond milk and allow to cook away for at least 6–8 minutes, lastly add the organic spinach, allow to wilt for 30 seconds, then serve.

Tasty Turkey Balls

Prep time: 8 mins
Cooking time: 20 mins
Serves: 3–4

Ingredients

- 1 pack organic turkey mince *(400g)*
- 2 tbsp tomato puree
- Handful fresh coriander – diced
- Fresh basil – diced
- 1 tbsp coconut oil

Method

Preheat the oven to 180°C; in a mixing bowl add the turkey mince, tomato puree and diced herbs. Mix well, then roll into small balls (slightly smaller then a golf ball).

To help them set and if you have time, place them in the fridge for at least 10 minutes.

In a pan, heat the coconut oil and gently fry on each side for 1–2 minutes, once brown all over place them into the oven for 15 minutes to finish cooking.

TMH tips
I served this at one of TMH Supper Clubs and they were a big hit! They said these are great to keep in the fridge for a Protein Snack.

HIGH PROTEIN
700% GUARANTEE

Homemade Chicken Liver Pâté

Prep time: 15 mins
Cooking time: 10 mins
Serves: 4–6

Ingredients

- 1 pack of organic chicken livers/or fresh from your local butcher
- 3 shallots – diced
- 40ml cranberry juice – I use the brand Biona
- 2 springs rosemary
- 50g organic butter

Method

Wash the livers and remove any cavity parts, then dice.

Heat 1 teaspoon of coconut oil in a pan and fry the diced shallots and diced rosemary for 5 minutes until they are soft and sweet.

Add the cranberry juice and simmer for a few minutes.

Remove the mixture and add them to a blender.

Place the livers back in the pan and fry for a few minutes on each side

TMH tips Organic Chicken livers are a brilliant source of folate, which is important for fertility

(don't over cook them otherwise you won't get a smooth texture). Season.

Once cooked, place them into the blender with the butter and blend until smooth.

Set in the fridge.

Now this dish may not look the best, but trust me it tastes absolutely delicious and you will never go back to store bought ones!

ONE POT WONDER

KEEP IT
Slow

Healthy
Lifestyle

Cashew AND Coconut Curry

Prep time: 8 mins
Cooking time: 20 mins
Serves: 3–4

Ingredients

For the Curry Powder

- 1 tbsp ground cumin
- 1 tbsp ground curry powder
- 1 tbsp ground coriander
- 1 tbsp ground cayenne pepper
- 1 tbsp coconut oil or ghee
- 1 tin of organic tomatoes
- 3 tbsp greek/plain yoghurt *(you can use coconut cream too)*
- 2 red onions – diced
- 2 handfuls fresh coriander
- 2 chicken breasts – sliced
- Either 150g cashews or 3 tbsp cashew nut butter
- 3 tbsp fresh coconut – ideally shredded *(this is a bit messy but well worth it)*

TMH tips

Cayenne pepper – Over 90 trials have been performed to evaluate the capsaicin in cayenne to determine its effectiveness as a weight loss aid and it was proven it reduces appetite. It helps break down fats.

Method

Add all the dry spices together into a bowl and mix well. In a large pan, fry the onions in the coconut oil until they are soft, then add the curry powder mixture and fry for a few minutes.

Add the sliced chicken breasts to the pan and fry on each side for a few minutes, then add the freshly diced coriander and the tin of tomatoes and simmer for 10 minutes.

After the 10 minutes, if you have whole cashew nuts, place them in the blender and blitz, then stir them into the mixture. If you are using cashew nut butter then add this straight into the mixture along with half of the shredded coconut.

Cook for 2 minutes, then serve.

Sprinkle some fresh coconut on top.

Spiced Paleo Butternut Squash Soup

Prep time: 15 mins
Cooking time: 40 mins
Serves: 4–6

Ingredients

- 1 large butternut squash *(or if you are in a hurry pre-diced squash – we all need some help sometimes)*
- 3 carrots – peeled
- 600ml gluten-free stock
- 150ml coconut milk
- 1 tbsp turmeric powder
- 1 tsp cinnamon
- 1 tbsp melted coconut oil
- Seasoning

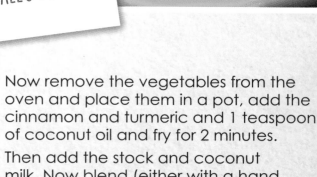

PALEO FOOD

Method

Preheat the oven to 180°C, then slice the carrots and butternut squash lengthways, scoop out the seeds (don't throw them away) lay the veg onto the tray, season, pour the melted coconut oil over them and roast for 30 minutes.

Now remove the vegetables from the oven and place them in a pot, add the cinnamon and turmeric and 1 teaspoon of coconut oil and fry for 2 minutes.

Then add the stock and coconut milk. Now blend (either with a hand blender or in a blender). Finally warm the soup thoroughly and serve with some of your toasted seeds.

Aubergine and Mozzarella Lasagne

Prep time: 10 mins
Cooking time: 30 mins
Serves: 4

Ingredients

- 1 pack organic beef mince
- 1 tin organic tomatoes
- 2 large aubergines – sliced lengthways
- Buffalo mozzarella – sliced
- 3 plum tomatoes
- 1 tsp smoked paprika
- Fresh basil
- 1 onion – diced

Method

Preheat the oven to 180°C, then over a medium heat gently fry the onion and paprika for a minute, then add in the beef mince. Then add the tin of tomatoes and fresh basil and allow to simmer for 5 minutes. In the meantime heat a griddle pan, and grill the sliced aubergine slices for 2 minutes on each side, until they are slightly char-grilled.

In a casserole dish, layer the mince first, then lay half of the aubergines on top, finally layer with some mozzarella and repeat the process again. The top layer should be sliced fresh plum tomatoes, topped with mozzarella with fresh basil on top, then bake in the oven for 30 minutes.

TMH Sweet Potato Cottage Pie

Prep time: 15 mins

Cooking time: 55 mins.

Serves: 2–3 Even Ed gets his own TMH Cottage Pie when we go on holiday

Ingredients

- 500g ground organic mince
- 4 sweet potatoes – peeled
- 1 onion – diced
- 1 tin organic tomatoes
- Fresh rosemary – diced
- Fresh basil – diced
- 1 tbsp organic butter *(optional)*

Method

Preheat the oven to 180°C.

Peel the potatoes, then place them into a pan of water over a medium heat and boil for 10–15 minutes.

In the meantime, heat a little coconut oil in a frying pan and fry the onion until soft. Add the rosemary and basil then add the mince and cook until brown. Next, add the tinned tomatoes. Top with 100ml of water, season then simmer for 10 minutes.

In my last book this recipe was such a hit with Butternut squash and Carrot that I decided to just tweak it with Sweet Potato.

Remove the sweet potato, season then add a little organic butter and mash until smooth.

In a casserole dish, layer the mince at the bottom then evenly spread the mash on top, spike with a fork and cook for 40 minutes.

Garlic AND Lemon Roasted Chicken Pot

Prep time: 10 mins
Cooking time: 75–90 mins
Serves: 2–3

Ingredients

- 1 organic chicken
- 2 unwaxed lemons
- 2 garlic cloves
- 1 orange
- 6 carrots – peeled
- 2 sprigs fresh rosemary
- 2 tbsp organic butter
- 6 carrots – halved
- 2 red onions – diced
- 2 sweet potatoes – diced
- 2 white potatoes – peeled
- 1 tbsp coconut oil

TMH tips

Keep the vegetables nice and chunky, so they don't overcook.

Cooking Guide for Chickens
Cooking 20 minutes per lb (450g) plus an extra 10-20 minutes.

This is great for a busy mid-week dinner.

Fruit producers tend to spray the skin of citrus fruits with a thin layer of wax after the fruit is harvested. This is done to keep the skin of the fruit looking fresh and provides some protection for the skin during transit. It also adds a shine.

Method

Preheat the oven to 180°C, then in a bowl mix the butter, rosemary, garlic, and juice from 1 lemon, season and mix well into a paste. Rub this all over the chicken.

Place the other lemon and orange inside the bird, dice all your vegetables then lay in the bottom of the roasting tray and sprinkle with the rosemary, lay the chicken on top of the vegetables and roast for the desired time on the instructions.

Cover with foil for the first 30 minutes, then remove for the remaining cooking time.

Good Old Fashioned Chicken Soup

Prep time: 15 mins

Cooking time:
Minimum 2 hours

Serves: 4–5

Ingredients

- 4 organic chicken drumsticks
- 4 organic chicken thighs *(they must have the bones in)*
- 4 carrots – peeled
- 3 leeks
- 6 sticks of celery
- 500ml water
- Fresh turmeric 1 inch *(I get this locally from my thai shop, but if you can't then just use the powder)* 4 tbsp turmeric powder
- 2 garlic cloves – sliced
- 4 rosemary sprigs
- 1 tbsp coconut oil
- Fresh coriander

TMH tips You want to slow cook the chicken to release all the goodness from the bones

Method

Firstly, remove the skin from the chicken pieces, then in a large pan heat the coconut oil, add sliced garlic, diced rosemary and turmeric. If you are using fresh turmeric then I recommend that you put some gloves on first and grate it into the pan. If not add the powder.

Now add the carrots, celery, leeks and brown for 5 minutes, add the chicken pieces and brown on each side. Now add the water, place the lid on and either cook on a low hob for 2 hours, or place in the oven for at least 2–3 hours. You may need to check that there is enough liquid in the pan.

CELERY

LOW CALORIES

HIGH FIBER

HIGH FOLATE

VITAMIN **A**

VITAMIN **C**

VITAMIN **K**

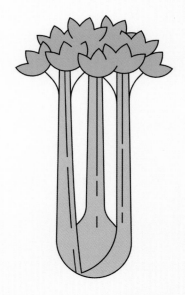

HEALTH BENEFITS

TMH tips

When I am feeling under the weather, then this is my "go to dish" to make me feel SSOOO much better. This is because it helps stop mucus from forming so can relieve cold and flu symptoms!!

Remove the dish from the hob or oven and allow to cool enough so you are able to handle the chicken. You now need to remove the chicken, and carefully remove any bones from the broth, throw the bones away and place the shredded chicken into a separate bowl. Now place the vegetables and broth mix and blend until it is nice and thick and it will look more like a soup.

Lastly return the soup back to the pan, add the shredded chicken and cook for 5–10 minutes until hot.

Serve with fresh coriander.

FISH

Fish meal

OMEGA 3
HIGH IN
MEGA 3 ✓
HIGH I
OMEGA
OMEGA 3. OMEGA 3 ✓
HIGH II

Garlic *and* Rosemary Salmon Supper

Prep time: 5 mins
Cooking time: 12–15 mins
Serves: 2

Ingredients

- 2 wild salmon fillets *(not farmed)*
- 1 tsp of cajun spice
- 2 sprigs fresh rosemary
- 2 garlic cloves – sliced
- 1 lemon
- 2 tbsp flaked almonds
- 1 tbsp organic butter

Method

If you have time before, then marinate the salmon first in a bag with the sliced garlic, diced rosemary, cajun spice, and 1 teaspoon of olive oil. If not then preheat the oven to 180°C, place the salmon fillets in some parchment paper and lay the garlic, rosemary, flaked almonds and lemon on top. Season the butter then add into the parcel, fold the edges, make a parcel then roast for 12–15 minutes.

 TMH tips

When butter comes from cows eating green grass, it contains high levels of conjugated linoleic acid (CLA), a compound that gives excellent protection against cancer and also helps your body build muscle rather than store fat.

106

Lemon, Chive AND Caper Cod Parcels

Prep time: 5 mins
Cooking time: 15 mins
Serves: 2

Ingredients

- 2 white fish fillets – I use cod
- 2 lemons
- 3 tbsp capers – diced
- 1 tbsp chives – diced

Method

Preheat the oven to 180°C, and marinate the fish in the juice of the 1 lemon, diced chives and capers. Now place the fish onto two squares of parchment paper and lay the other sliced lemon on top. Wrap the fish up in the paper and cook for 10–12 minutes. We served ours on a bed of rice and roasted peppers.

Spice Rubbed Salmon – Perfect Midweek Meal

Prep time: 5 mins
Cooking time: 6 mins
Serves: 2

Ingredients

- 1 tbsp garam masala
- 1 tbsp cumin powder
- 1 tbsp coriander powder
- 1 tbsp paprika
- 1 fresh lime – sliced
- 2 salmon fillets *(sustainably sourced where possible)*

Method

Preheat the oven to 180ºC, then in a bowl mix all the spices together. Lightly oil the fish then rub the spices into the salmon.

On a medium heat place a pan with no oil and seal the salmon for 1 minute on each side, now place in the oven, layer the zest on top and bake for 6 minutes. This way you will get a perfectly cooked fish without burning the skin.

Zesty Tuna Salad

Prep time: 15 mins
Cooking time: 5 mins
Serves: 2

Ingredients

- 2 tuna steaks
- 4 handfuls spinach leaves
- Handful chopped mint
- ¼ cucumber – grated
- 2 tbsp sesame seeds
- 2 plum tomatoes – diced
- ½ avocado

Dressing & marinade

- 4 tbsp olive oil
- 1 juice fresh lime
- 1 fresh chilli – diced

TMH tips

Sesame seeds are incredibly rich sources of many essential minerals. Calcium, iron, manganese, zinc, magnesium, selenium, and copper are especially concentrated in sesame seeds.

Method

Marinate the tuna steak in half the marinade for at least 15 minutes, in the meantime prepare the salad by adding everything into one large bowl and stir.

Heat a griddle pan over a medium heat then add the marinated tuna and fry on each side for 1–3 minutes.

Serve your salad then flake the tuna on top.

Crispy Calamari

Prep time: 5 mins
Cooking time: 8–10 mins
Serves: 3–4

Ingredients

- 2 fresh squid tubes, sliced into rings
- 200g rice flour
- Pinch sea salt
- Pinch cayenne pepper and paprika
- 2 eggs

Method

In a bowl whisk the eggs and in a separate bowl mix the flour and season with the spices. Coat the rings with the flour mix, then dip them into the egg mixture.

In a pan over a medium/high heat melt 3 tablespoons of coconut oil and fry for 2–3 minutes, turning occasionally.

Once cooked, squeeze some lemon juice and sea salt and enjoy!

This was taken on the Racha Island in Barbados, where we had the most delicious fresh fish.

110

Fried Cajun Crispy Prawns

Prep time: 5 mins
Cooking time: 3 mins
Serves: 2

Ingredients

- 12 fresh prawns
- ½ cup coconut flour
- 1 egg
- ½ cup almond milk
- 1 teaspoon cajun seasoning
- 3 tbsp coconut oil

Method

Mix all the ingredients together in a bowl to make the batter, then add the washed and peeled prawns into the batter and coat thoroughly. In a small pan heat the coconut oil until it is very hot (mine only took 45 seconds). Then gently add the prawns and allow to brown for a few minutes then remove from the pan. Great as a dinner party snack.

FRESH SEAFOOD
For Prawn Lovers
TODAY'S CATCH

Pan Fried Fish and Homemade Red Pepper Pesto

Prep time: 5 mins
Cooking time: 6 mins
Serves: 2

Ingredients

- 2 white fish fillets
- 2 red peppers
- 4 large tomatoes
- 1 tbsp coconut oil
- Organic butter
- 1 onion – diced
- Fresh basil

TMH tips Ancient herbalists believed placing basil leaves on the bites or stings of insects would draw out the poison. Today's herbalists recommend its use as a digestive and anti-gas aid.

Method

Preheat the oven to 180°C, then add the coconut oil to a baking tray, place in the oven and melt. Then add the diced tomatoes, peppers and onions and roast for 20 minutes.

Remove from the oven and place them into a blender, add the fresh basil and seasoning and blend until smooth.

In the meantime, heat a small pan with ½ teaspoon of organic butter, season your fish then place it into the pan. It depends on the thickness of your fish but for example a sea bass fillet will take a few minutes on each side. Turn over and baste with the butter.

Serve alongside some green vegetables and add the pesto on top of the fish.

VEGETARIAN

Vegetarian
Menu

HEALT
NATU

Lemongrass

Eucal

Peppermint

Rosemary

NATURAL
VEGETARIAN
PRODUCT

✔ VEGETARIAN
100% NATURAL

VEGETARIAN
100% NATURAL

VEGETARIAN VEGETARIAN

Glorious Green Soup

Prep time: 10 mins
Cooking time: 20 mins
Serves: 2

Ingredients

- 1 whole broccoli
- 2 cloves crushed garlic
- 1 tsp coconut oil
- 2 handfuls spinach
- 300ml stock *(vegetable)*
- 2 tbsp yoghurt if needed

Method

In a pan heat the coconut oil and fry the garlic until soft. Now add the stock and the broccoli and allow to simmer for 10 minutes. Add the spinach at the very end.

Add all the ingredients into a blender and blitz until smooth, add the yoghurt if you wish.

Fabulous Falafels

Prep time: 10 mins
Cooking time: 15 mins
Serves: 2–3

Ingredients

- Either 1 tin chick peas or 200g raw chick peas *(soaked overnight)*
- 2 handfuls – diced coriander
- Juice ½ lemon
- 1 tbsp harrisa paste
- 30g gluten-free porridge oats
- 1 tbsp coconut oil
- 2 tbsp olive oil
- Seasoning

Method

In a blender add the chickpeas, diced coriander, paste, lemon juice, coconut oil, olive oil, porridge oats and blend until smooth. (approx. 1 minute)

Season to your taste, then heat 1 tablespoon of coconut oil in a pan over a medium heat.

Make small burger shape falafels patties and gently fry them on each side for 3–4 minutes.

Serve and enjoy.

Egg Quinoa Salad

Prep time: 5 mins
Cooking time: 15 mins
Serves: 2

Don't Worry Be Happy

Ingredients

- 100g of quinoa
- 1 carrot – grated
- ½ lettuce – diced thinly
- 4 boiled eggs
- 1 red pepper – sliced
- 1 red chilli – diced
- 50g peas – cooked
- 1 tbsp olive oil
- 1 tbsp balsamic vinegar

 TMH tips Quinoa works really well with lots of ingredients, so enjoy making some of your own creations.

· Method

In a pan of water, add the quinoa and gently simmer for approx. 10 minutes until cooked through.

In the mean time boil the eggs, and prepare the remaining salad. In a bowl mix the lettuce, carrot, chillis, peas pepper, olive oil and balsamic vinegar and mix well.

Once the quinoa has been drained and cooled add to the salad, mix well then lay your boiled eggs on top.

Roasted Beetroot AND Cumin Salad

Prep time: 5 mins
Cooking time: 30–40 mins
Serves: 2–3

Ingredients

- 2 large beetroots
- 2 tbsp cumin seeds
- 2 tbsp coconut oil

Method

Preheat the oven to 180°C, and add the coconut oil on a tray to melt in the oven. Once it has melted, dice the beetroot into quarters, place into some foil, sprinkle with the cumin seeds and coconut oil, season well then wrap up. Roast for at least 30-40 minutes.

TMH tips

You can't beat fresh beetroot and I am lucky enough to get it from my Mum and Dad's allotment. My mum boils it first then drops it off to me – Perfect!

A lovely little Veg shop on our trip to the Cotswolds!

Protein Packed Supper

Prep time: 5 mins
Cooking time: 15 mins
Serves: 2

Ingredients

- 1 cup of quinoa (*I like the red ones*)
- 2 handfuls mint
- Cucumber – diced
- 4 radishes – diced
- 12 almonds
- 12 cashew nuts
- Fresh coriander – diced
- Juice of 1 lemon

Method

In a pan of water, add the quinoa and gently simmer for approx. 10 minutes until cooked through.

Heat 1 teaspoon of coconut oil in a pan and gently toast the almonds and cashew nuts for a few minutes.

Once the quinoa has cooked and cooled, mix in the diced mint, toasted nuts, cucumber, radishes, and the juice of the lemon.

Roasted Tomato and Pepper Soup

Prep time: 5 mins
Cooking time: 30 mins
Serves: 2

Ingredients

- 8 large vine tomatoes
- 2 large red peppers
- 1 small red onion
- 1 garlic clove – peeled
- 200ml organic vegetable stock
- Fresh basil

Method

Preheat oven to 180°C, then place the diced tomatoes, garlic, peppers and onions onto a baking tray, drizzle with olive oil and fresh basil and roast for 25 minutes. Once cooled, place them into a blender and blend for a minute. Place the mixture into a pan, add 200ml of vegetable stock and simmer for 5–8 minutes. Serve with fresh basil and enjoy.

Notes...

SIDES

GROWN Locally

FARM Fresh

Garlic Cauliflower Mash

Prep time: 3 mins
Cooking time: 8–10 mins
Serves: 2–3

Ingredients

- 1 cauliflower
- 1 tsp coconut oil
- 60ml coconut milk
- 2 cloves garlic – crushed
- Seasoning

Method

Bring a large pot of water to a boil over a high heat. Dice the cauliflower into florets and place in the boiling water and cook for anywhere between approx. 8–10 minutes, until the cauliflower is tender. Strain the cauliflower from the water and place back into the pot. Add the cooking oil, coconut milk, garlic, salt and pepper. Mash the mixture by using a hand blender, or pour everything into a blender. Blend until smooth in texture.

Roasted Butternut Squash

Prep time: 10 mins
Cooking time: 40 mins
Serves: 3

Ingredients

- 1 butternut squash – peeled and diced
- 1 tbsp coconut oil
- 2 garlic cloves – crushed
- Black pepper

Method

Preheat the oven to 180°C, then dice and peel the butternut squash (I know it can be hard work) but well worth it. Crush the garlic cloves, but keeping them whole, lay them in the roasting tray then add the coconut oil and melt for 1 minute in the oven. Now add the diced squash, ensure they are all evenly coated in the oil and roast for 40 minutes.

Chargrilled Garlic Asparagus

Prep time: 2 mins
Cooking time: 3 mins
Serves: 2

Ingredients

- Bunch of asparagus
- 2 garlic cloves – crushed
- 1 tbsp organic butter or you can use coconut oil
- Seasoning

 TMH tips   The british asparagus season, from May to June

Method

Place the butter in a bowl, then add the crushed garlic to the butter and mix well. Heat a griddle pan over a medium heat, add the butter then the asparagus spears. Grill on each side for 60 seconds.

Drizzle with the remaining butter and serve.

Grilled Chilli Spiced Courgette

Prep time: 2 mins
Cooking time: 8 mins
Serves: 2

Ingredients

- 1 courgette – sliced lengthways
- 1 tbsp olive oil
- 1 red chilli – diced
- Fresh coriander – diced
- Rocket leaves

 **TMH tips** Fresh salad rocket is a very good source of folates, so great for pregnant women.

Method

Drizzle the olive oil, chilli and coriander over the sliced courgettes and ensure they are all evenly coated. Heat a griddle pan over a medium heat and grill on each side for 3–4 minutes.

Serve on a bed of fresh rocket.

Sauteed Sesame Seed Spinach

Prep time: 5 mins
Cooking time: 1 min
Serves: 2

Ingredients

- 8 handfuls spinach leaves
- 4 tbsp sesame seeds
- 1 tbsp coconut oil

Method

Heat the coconut oil in a pan, add the spinach, allow to wilt for 15 seconds, add the sesame seeds and serve.

Crispy Apple AND Red Cabbage

Prep time: 10 mins
Cooking time: 0 mins
Serves: 2–3

Ingredients

- 1 red cabbage – diced thinly
- 2 apples – peeled and chopped
- 2 tbsp apple cider vinegar
- Juice ½ lemon
- 4 tbsp olive oil
- Fresh coriander
- Sea salt and black pepper

Method

In a small bowl mix the olive oil, apple cider vinegar and lemon juice and season. Dice the cabbage and apple, add both into a bowl, then pour the dressing over and mix well. Sprinkle with coriander and serve.

TMH tips

Vinegar is one of the best natural agents for removing certain pesticides and bacteria from your fresh produce. Mix 90% water and 10% vinegar to wash your fruits and vegetables (not berries)

Great Green Salad

Prep time: 2 mins
Cooking time: 2 mins
Serves: 2

Ingredients

- Spinach leaves
- 6 red cherry tomatoes
- 2 tbsp olive oil
- Fresh basil leaves

Method

Place all the ingredients into a bowl and enjoy the simple and delicious side salad.

Boosting Broccoli Salad

Prep time: 5 mins
Cooking time: 10 mins
Serves: 2

Ingredients

- 6 broccoli florettes
- 6 olives
- ½ cucumber – diced
- 8 cherry tomatoes
- 1 red onion – diced
- Spinach leaves
- Fresh basil leaves
- 2 tbsp olive oil

Method

Steam the broccoli florettes for
3–5 minutes, in the meantime in
a large bowl mix the spinach,
basil, cucumber, olives, red onion
and tomatoes. Add the broccoli,
drizzle with olive oil and mix well.

nutritional food

Balsamic Glazed Green Bean Salad

Prep time: 3 mins
Cooking time: 3 mins
Serves: 2

Ingredients

- 1 pack of green beans
- 1 red onion – diced
- 3 tbsp balsamic vinegar
- 1 tsp coconut oil

TMH tips

Balsamic vinegar's tangy and sweet properties make it an adaptable ingredient, but it is also a nutritional powerhouse, Balsamic vinegar contains electrolytes including calcium, magnesium, zinc, phosphorus, potassium and sodium.

Method

In a pan, add the coconut oil and melt over medium heat. Add the onion and green beans and fry for 3 minutes, then add the balsamic vinegar and fry for 30 seconds, making sure they are all coated.

Serve – This is great with some crushed nuts sprinkled on top.

Roasted Root Veg

Prep time: 5 mins
Cooking time: 40 mins
Serves: 2–3

Ingredients

- 3 carrots – peeled
- ½ butternut squash – diced
- 4 parsnips – peeled
- Fresh rosemary – diced
- 1 tbsp coconut oil
- Sea salt

Butternut squash is composed of many vital poly-phenolic anti-oxidants and vitamins and high levels of Vitamin A

Method

Preheat the oven to 180°C, peel and dice the vegetables, place the carrots and parsnips in a pan of water and simmer for 10 minutes until soft. Heat the coconut oil in a roasting tray and melt in the oven, now add the part boiled carrots, parsnips, and butternut squash and rosemary. Season with sea salt and roast for 40 minutes.

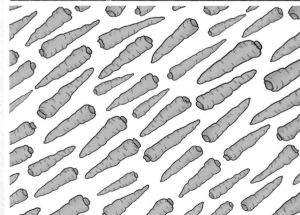

Herby Roasted Sweet Potato AND Onions

Prep time: 5 mins
Cooking time: 35 mins
Serves: 2

Ingredients

- 2 sweet potatoes – peeled and diced into cubes
- 2 garlic cloves
- 2 white onions – diced
- Fresh thyme
- 1 tbsp coconut oil

Method

Preheat the oven to 180°C, then dice and peel your sweet potatoes into cubes. Peel and slice the garlic and dice the fresh thyme. Heat the coconut oil in a roasting tray for 1 minute until it melts, then add the sweet potato, sliced garlic and diced thyme and coat well. Roast for 35 minutes and serve.

DIPS AND SAUCES

OLIVE

★ ★ ★ ★ ★

OIL

Garlic Avocado Dip

Prep time: 5 mins
Cooking time: 0! Woo-hoo
Serves: 2

Ingredients

- 1 avocado
- Juice ½ orange
- 1 garlic clove *(optional)*
- 100ml coconut/almond milk or water
- Seasoning

Method

Place all the ingredients into a blender and blend until a smooth creamy texture.

Home-made Mayonnaise

Prep time: 10 mins
Cooking time: 0
Serves: 4–6

Ingredients

- 2 egg yolks
- 1 tsp mustard *(this is optional)*
- 3 tsp lemon juice
- ½ cup olive oil

Method

Put the yolks in a bowl (blender, food processor) with the mustard, if using add 1 teaspoon lemon juice and mix those ingredients together;

Start whisking vigorously (blender or food processor on low) while dripping the oil very slowly, even drop by drop in the beginning. Now you are creating an emulsion and if you put too much oil in at once it will separate and will be very hard to save. Whisk non-stop.

Apple Cider AND Honey Salad Dressing

Prep time: 2 mins
Cooking time: 0 mins
Serves: 2

Ingredients

- 6 tbsp organic olive oil
- 3 tbsp apple cider vinegar
- 1 tbsp honey
- Pinch of sea salt and pepper

Method

Combine the honey, cider vinegar and seasoning and stir, then add the olive oil. Stir well, then drizzle over your salad.

you *are* amazing

Chilli-lime Dressing

Prep time: 5 mins
Cooking time: 0
Serves: 2

Ingredients

- 6 tbsp organic olive oil
- 1 tsp honey
- 1 red chilli – diced thinly
- Juice from 1 lime
- Seasoning

Method

Blend all the ingredients together, mix very well and then use it either as a salad dressing or as a great marinade for chicken.

Paleo Sticky Sweet Chilli Dip

Prep time: 5 mins
Cooking time: 0 mins
Serves: 3–4

Ingredients

- 5 tbsp apple cider vinegar
- 2 garlic cloves – crushed
- 2 tbsp honey
- 2 red chillies – diced
- 1 tsp arrowroot *(a gluten-free thickening agent found in the baking aisle)*
- 1 tsp fresh ginger – grated
- Pinch of sea salt
- ¼ tsp coconut oil
- ½ tsp cayenne pepper

Method

Crush the garlic and ginger through a crusher so you have a paste, then in a saucepan fry the coconut oil, vinegar, ginger, garlic, chillies, honey and cayenne pepper. Then add the arrowroot and stir until it is all absorbed.

Now cook for at least 1–2 minutes until it thickens.

Now all you need to do is either drizzle over your favourite meal, or dunk some sweet potato fries in them!

Spicy Salsa

Prep time: 5 mins
Cooking time: 0 mins
Serves: 3–4

Ingredients

- 5 medium tomatoes
- 1 red onion
- 150ml balsamic vinegar
- 1–2 jalapenos
- ½ cup of chopped fresh coriander
- Salt and pepper
- 1 tbsp olive oil
- Lemon juice

Method

Dice the tomatoes, onion, and jalapenos, add to a bowl then add the other ingredients, combine them all together and serve.

TMH tips

The health benefits of coriander include its use in the treatment of skin inflammation, high cholesterol levels, diarrhoea, mouth ulcers, anaemia, indigestion, menstrual disorders, smallpox, conjunctivitis, skin disorders, and blood sugar disorders, while also benefiting eye care.

Garlic Pesto

Prep time: 10 mins
Cooking time: 0 mins
Serves: 2–3

Ingredients

- 8 handfuls fresh spinach
- 1 handful fresh basil leaves
- 8 tbsp olive oil
- 150g pine nuts
- 2 garlic cloves
- Sea salt
- 1 tsp coconut oil

Method

Heat the coconut oil in a skillet and add the pine nuts, gently fry them for a few minutes, until just golden.

Now add your spinach, basil, garlic, olive oil, pine nuts and sea salt to a blender and blend until smooth.

This can be stored for a few days in the fridge.

Chicken Bone Broth

Prep time: 20 mins

Cooking time:
Minimum 4 hours

Serves: ??

Ingredients

- Chicken necks and feet
- Enough water to cover the chicken
- 3 tbsp apple cider vinegar
- Sea salt and ground black pepper
- 2 bay leaves
- 2 garlic cloves
- Vegetables of choice – carrots, leeks, garlic, onions, etc.

Method

Place all ingredients into a stockpot and add enough water until chicken is submerged.

Turn setting to high and cook for 4 hours, then reduce to simmer on low for the remaining time.

 TMH tips Beef Bones can take 24-48 hours

 TMH tips Once cooled there will be a layer of hard fat on the top, this layer protects the broth. Discard this before using the broth.

Notes...

SNACKS

DO SOMETHING AWESOME RIGHT NOW

Spread Love! AND LOVE WILL SPREAD

Cranberry AND Almond Butter Bars

Prep time: 10 mins
Cooking time: 0
Serves: 2–3

Ingredients

- 3 tbsp almond butter
- 100g dried cranberries
- 5 figs *(or you could use dates)*
- 1 scoop TMH Vanilla Protein powder

Method

Place all the ingredients into a blender and blitz until smooth.

Take 1 tablespoon of the mixture and roll into a long bar shape (approx. 3 inches)

Place the bar into some cling film, wrap and set in the freezer for 15 minutes.

Unwrap them, then either enjoy them straight away or roll them in your favourite toppings.

After Eight Protein Balls

Prep time: 10 mins
Chilling time: 10 mins (if you can wait that long!)
Serves: 2–3

Ingredients

- 2 scoops TMH vanilla protein
- 150g ground almonds
- 1 tsp coconut oil
- 8 dates
- 1 tbsp cocoa powder
- 2 tbsp almond butter
- 5 fresh mint leaves *(optional)*
- 6 tbsp desiccated coconut
- 100ml almond milk

Method

In a blender mix the dates and almond milk first to a paste. Then add the ground almonds, almond butter, coconut oil, cocoa powder, protein powder and fresh mint and blend. Once all combined, scoop 1 tablespoon at a time, roll them into a ball and roll them in the desiccated coconut. Allow to set in the fridge for at least 10 minutes.

For Amanda Stevens!!

Yep another chocolate and mint combination that I am sure you will love

Sesame and Almond Crackers

Prep time: 10 mins
Cooking time: 12–15 mins
Serves: 2–3

Ingredients

- 400g almonds
- 5 tbsp mixed seeds TMH Tip – I like the sesame, chia and linseed mix
- 1 egg
- 2 tbsp olive oil
- 1 tsp sea salt

Method

Preheat the oven to 180°. Place the almonds into a blender and blitz, place into a mixing bowl. Mix in the eggs, olive oil, salt and 3 tablespoons of the seeds and mix well.

Place the mixture onto a sheet of greaseproof paper, and place another sheet on top. Then roll the mixture out until it is a few mm's thick.

Cut the desired shapes for your crackers, sprinkle the other 2 tablespoons of seeds on top.

Place them in the oven for

12–15 minutes until crispy, remove from the oven and allow to cool and let any excess oil dry out.

146

Cinnamon Roasted Pecans

Prep time: 4 hours
Cooking time: 30 mins
Serves: 2–3

Ingredients

- 250g pecans
- 1 tbsp sea salt *(himalayan rock salt)*
  TMH Tip – From health stores!
- 1 tsp cinnamon
- 1 tbsp coconut oil

Method

Place the pecans in a bowl of water then add the sea salt and soak for at least 3 hours. Preheat the oven to 100°C then add the coconut oil to a roasting tray and place it into the oven to melt. Pat the pecans dry then sprinkle the cinnamon over them. Place these on the tray and make sure they all evenly coated in the oil and roast for 30 minutes.

Wasabi Almonds

Prep time: 15 mins
Cooking time: 20 mins
Serves: 3–4

Ingredients

- 250g almonds with the skin on
- 3 tbsp wasabi paste *(or ½ tsp wasabi powder)*
- 1 egg white
- 1 tbsp arrowroot

Method

Preheat the oven to 100°C, then soak the almonds in water for 15 minutes. Drain them in a bowl and roll them in the arrowroot, then in a bowl whisk the egg white until frothy, add the almonds and cover them all. Remove from the egg mixture and lastly marinate the almonds in the wasabi paste. Coat well then bake for at least 20 minutes.

Roasted Chestnuts

Prep time: 5 mins
Cooking time: 15 mins
Serves: 2–3

Ingredients

• 1 bag chestnuts

Method

Score the chestnuts on the outside with a cross, place on a baking tray and roast for 15 minutes.

Allow to cool slightly then peel and enjoy.

This is such a fond food memory, as my dad used to get some hot roasted chestnuts at Fenchurch Street Station and they would stay warm in his pocket all the way home for my mum and I to enjoy.

Perfect Prawn Bellinis

Prep time: 5 mins
Cooking time: 5 mins
Serves: 2–3

Ingredients

- 2 eggs
- 5 tbsp coconut flour
- Seasoning
- ½ tsp coconut oil
- Fresh prawns
- Fresh smoked salmon
- Homemade mayonnaise
- 8 tbsp olive oil
- Seasoning
- Lemon juice
- 2 eggs

Method

Place the eggs into a blender and blend for 2 minutes, then add the olive oil, lemon juice seasoning and blend for a further 2–5 minutes. You want to aim for a rich creamy texture.

Bellini's
Place the eggs into a bowl and whisk for 2 minutes. Then add the flour and season, stir well until it forms a batter. Then heat the coconut oil into a pan over a medium heat and add 1 tablespoon at a time, allow the shapes to form even sized circles and fry for 2 minutes each side. Allow to cool for a few minutes.

Now spread your homemade mayonnaise on to the Bellinis, and finally top with your prawns and fresh chives.

TREATS

Enjoy the little Things

I love Rick Stein's style of cooking so we all stayed in his Hotel for a weekend in Cornwall. (including Eddie)

Baked with Love By:

Better than Nutella Brownie!

Prep time: 5 mins
Cooking time: 35 mins
(be patient, its worth it)
Serves: 3–4

Ingredients

- 3 tbsp coconut oil
- 3 eggs
- 50g banana flour *(don't worry you could use ground porridge oats instead)*
- 4 tbsp cocoa powder
- 100g raw or dark chocolate – melted
- 200g coconut palm sugar
- 1 tsp gluten-free baking powder
- 150g chopped hazelnuts (you can swap and use walnuts, but I like hazelnuts as it replicates the Nutella flavour)

Method

Preheat the oven to 180°C and grease and line a baking tray and oil with coconut oil.

In a bowl mix the coconut sugar, cocoa powder, banana flour, melted dark chocolate and gluten-free baking powder until all combined.

Whisk the eggs, then add them to the bowl. Pour in the diced hazelnuts and stir gently. Pour the mixture into the tray and bake for 35 minutes.

Serve and enjoy with all your friends and family.

Banana Loaf

Prep time: 10 mins
Cooking time: 35 mins
Serves: 4–6

Ingredients

- 2 bananas
- 250g gluten-free self-raising flour
- 1 tsp gluten-free baking powder
- 3 eggs
- 250ml almond milk
- ½ tsp cinnamon
- 1 tsp coconut oil – for greasing
- Pinch of salt
- 4 tbsp honey

Method

Preheat the oven to 180°C and grease and line a bread tin with greaseproof paper and coconut oil.

In a large bowl mash the bananas until soft, then add the gluten-free flour, cinnamon, almond milk, baking powder and stir. In a small bowl mix together the eggs, salt and honey and once all combined add this to the flour bowl. Once all the mixture is combined together then pour into the bread tin and bake for 40 minutes.

Avocado AND Lime Tart

Prep time: 7 mins
Cooking time: 0 mins
Serves: 2

Ingredients

Topping
- 2 avocados
- 3 limes *(juice and zest)*
- 1 tbsp coconut oil
- 1 tbsp honey

Biscuit Base
- 8 tbsp ground almonds
- 2 tbsp seeds
- 2 tbsp chia seeds
- 2 tbsp honey

Method

Place all the base ingredients into a bowl and combine well, split the mixture and place in the bottom of two small tart dishes.

In a blender combine the avocados, lime juice and lime zest, honey and coconut oil and blend until smooth.

Scoop on top of the biscuit base and set in the fridge for 30 minutes.

I think the avocado mixture is a really lovely morning breakfast snack topped with berries and nuts!

Protein Packed Meringues

Prep time: 5 mins
Cooking time: 60 mins
Serves: 4

Ingredients

- 4 egg whites
- 2 scoops of TMH vanilla protein powder *(optional)*
- 50g xylitol
- Fresh strawberries to top
- Fresh organic cream or coconut cream

Method

Preheat the oven to 140°C and grease and line a tray with parchment paper.

In a large mixing bowl whisk the egg whites until they are stiff, gently sift and fold in the protein powder then add the xylitol 1 tbsp at a time and stir.

Spoon the mixture into a piping bag and pipe, small meringues, then place in the oven and bake for 60 minutes, allow to cool for as long as you can. Then top with either fresh whipped cream (or coconut cream) and top with fresh strawberries.

TMH tips

Xylitol. Pure xylitol comes in white crystals and looks and tastes like ordinary granulated sugar. This was the most natural substitute that I could find for meringues.

Raw Pecan Protein Bites

Prep time: 10 mins

Cooking time: setting time – 20 mins

Serves: 3–4

Ingredients

- 400g pecans blended until fine *(or your favourite nut)*
- 2 tbsp cocoa powder
- 2 tbsp TMH pure vanilla protein powder
- 50ml water
- 10 dates
- Pinch of sea salt
- 1 tsp of melted coconut oil

Method

Place the nuts into the blender first and blend. Then add the dates, cocoa powder, protein powder, melted coconut oil and water and blend until the mix starts to come together. Add more water if needed.

Place the mixture into a small greased baking tray, lay a layer of cling film over the top and roll out until smooth. Mark out the size shape bars that you want.

TMH Tip: I use a cookie cutter. Pop into the fridge to set for at least 20 minutes.

Chocolate and Peanut Butter Cups

Prep time: 5 mins
Cooking time: 5 mins
Serves: 6 (or 1 greedy Peanut butter lover)

Ingredients

- 1 bar of dark chocolate *(I used 85 % as I like it quite bitter)*
- 3 tbsp organic peanut butter *(or almond butter if you prefer)*.
- 2 tbsp coconut cream. If you would like it less bitter then you could add in more cream or use a lower % cocoa content, especially for children.

TMH tips — Almond Butter is my favourite

Method

Place a pan of water over a medium heat, then bring to a simmer.

Break the chocolate into small pieces, then place them into a glass bowl and melt slowly over the pan. Gradually add in the coconut cream until it is nice and glossy and keep stirring.

In a small muffin tray, place a small amount of chocolate in the bottom, then place ½ tsp of peanut butter in each section. Finally pour in the remaining chocolate until the peanut

butter is completely covered.

I like my chocolate cold, so I placed mine in the freezer to set for approx. 40 minutes, or you can have them more of a mousse consistency and set them in the fridge for a few hours.

Sticky Toffee Pudding

Prep time: 5 mins
Cooking time: 25 mins
Serves: 6

Ingredients

- 150g gluten-free flour
- 150g organic butter
- 150g coconut palm sugar
- 2 eggs
- 100g dates
- 100ml water
- 1 tsp gluten-free baking powder
- 1 tbsp maple syrup or honey

Toffee sauce

- 50g butter
- 2 tbsp coconut cream
- 25g coconut sugar

Method

Preheat oven to 180°C and grease a round cake tin dish with a small amount of butter. In a small pan, add the dates and water and simmer for a few minutes.

In a mixing bowl, combine the butter and coconut palm sugar then add in the egg, baking powder, gluten free flour and syrup. Now take the dates from the pan and mash them to a paste. Add them to the mixture, stir and pour into your greased dish.

Bake for 20-25 minutes.

Once the cake has cooled, you can make a super easy

Toffee sauce

See the next page for the toffee sauce recipe.

Toffee Sauce

Prep time: 2 mins
Cooking time: 3 mins
Serves: 4

Ingredients

- 50g organic butter
- 2 tbsp coconut cream
- 25g coconut sugar

Method

Place all the ingredients into a pan and bring to a simmer until all the sugar has dissolved and it is a lovely toffee texture.

Toffee Doughnuts

Prep time: 5 mins
Cooking time: 15 mins
Serves: 4–6

I love walking along our seafront in Leigh-on-Sea, and the smell of doughnuts always get me!! So I created these as they are far healthier

Ingredients

- 30g coconut flour – sieved
- 40g ground almonds
- ¼ tsp gluten-free baking powder
- ¼ tsp ground cinnamon
- 3 eggs
- 4 tbsp raw honey or (organic honey)
-

- 2 tbsp coconut oil (melted)
- 1 tbsp vanilla essence

For the topping

- 2 tbsp almond butter
- 2 tbsp honey
- or you can use the toffee sauce recipe on the other page

Method

Preheat the oven to 180°C and grease either 10 small or 4 large doughnut moulds with coconut oil and set aside.

Place the ground almonds, coconut flour, baking powder and cinnamon into a bowl and combine well.

In a separate large bowl, combine the eggs, vanilla, honey and melted coconut oil.

Now mix all the dry ingredients into the other bowl and stir until all the mixture is combined like a batter.

Now place the mixture into a piping bag and gently squeeze the mixture into the doughnut moulds.

Fill them to the top, but leave space for the mixture to rise into a round shape.

Lay them on a tray and bake them for approx. 15 minutes or until cooked all the way through.

Remove from the oven and allow to cool for 1–2 minutes before you start the topping.

Toffee Topping

In a pan over a medium heat add the nut butter and the honey and allow it to thicken for a few minutes whilst you are continually stirring. Be careful not to burn the sauce. Then dip each doughnut into the sauce and allow to cool and enjoy.

Sea Salt Cashew Chocolate Nut Bar

Prep time: 2 mins
Cooking time: 5 mins
Serves: 4–5

Ingredients

- 1½ cups cashew nuts
- ½ tsp sea salt
- 1 bar organic dark chocolate – 100g
- 1tsp coconut oil – for greasing
- 50ml almond milk

Method

Grease a baking tray and line with parchment paper (use the coconut oil to grease). Melt the chocolate in a bowl over a pan of water on a medium heat. Once the chocolate has melted then add the sea salt and almond milk and stir. Pour the mixture onto the parchment then sprinkle the cashews on top.

Set in the freezer for 30 mins, then you can store them in the fridge.

CACAO.
CHOCOLATE
chocolate

Gooey Chocolate Pudding

Prep time: 5 mins
Cooking time: 16 mins
Serves: 1 (well why share!) ☺

Ingredients

- 4 tbsp ground almonds
- 1 teaspoon cocoa powder
- 2 tbsp honey
- 1 egg
- ¼ tsp vanilla essence

Method

Grease a ramekin with coconut oil, then mix all the ingredients in a bowl until smooth. Pour in the ramekin and bake for 16–18 minutes at 180°C.

TMH tips For an extra treat, add 1 square of chocolate into the middle of the mix so it will be extra chocolatey

Life is short... Eat dessert first

Strawberry *AND* Pear Gooey Gluten-free Pie

This is really simple to make and tastes absolutely amazing and perfect for a Sunday Treat.

Prep time: 20 mins
Cooking time: 12–14 mins
Serves: 4

Ingredients

For the pie:
- 360g ground almonds
- 100ml maple syrup or honey
- 2 tbsp vanilla essence
- ½ tsp sea salt
- ½ tsp baking powder
- 3 tbsp coconut oil

For the filling
- 2 pears – peeled and diced
- 10 strawberries – washed and chopped
- 1 tsp cinnamon
- 4 tbsp water
- 100ml maple syrup or honey
- I also added in 1 tbsp rose water drops

This is my pie before the lid goes on, to show you how gooey it is.

Method

Preheat the oven to 180°C, grease a sheet of baking paper with coconut oil and the base of the pie dish (approx. 7–9 inches). Place the base of the pie dish onto the paper and draw around the edges in order for you to get the correct size to make the pie lid. In a bowl mix the ground almonds, sea salt and baking powder until well combined then add the maple syrup and coconut oil and stir until a thick paste. Split the mixture in half and spoon half of it on the pie base and gently press the mix down until the base is covered and the sides are slightly raised(I pinch the edges to do this). With the other half, lay it onto the baking paper and gently press down into the shape of the pie dish.

Place both dishes into the oven and bake for 12–14 mins, until golden, remove them from the oven and once the pastry lid has cooled slightly place it into the freezer and let it set for 15 minutes.

In the meantime in a pan over a medium heat add the pear and allow to cook for a few minutes, then add the strawberries, water, cinnamon (rose water optional) and maple syrup until it starts to get gooey (approx. 4 minutes). Then you can construct your pie, take your warm base and lay the pie filling on top, then gently place your set pie lid from the freezer on top.

The biscuit mix is also great just by itself.

Red Berry Protein Ice Cream

Prep time: 1 min
Cooking time: 0 min
Serves: 2

Ingredients

- 400g frozen mixed berries
- 2 tbsp coconut cream or 100ml coconut milk
- 1 scoop TMH pure protein *(or 1 tbsp honey)*

Method

Blend everything together until smooth.

Blueberry AND Coconut Ice Cream

Prep time: 2 mins
Cooking time: 0 mins
Serves: 1

Ingredients

- 400g frozen blueberries
- 2 tbsp coconut cream or 150ml coconut milk
- 1 scoop TMH pure protein *(or 1 tbsp honey)*
- Sprinkle of desiccated coconut for topping

Method

Blend everything together until smooth, if you want it smoother add more cream or milk. Serve and sprinkle with desiccated coconut.

Banana AND Honey Ice Cream

Prep time: 0 mins
Cooking time: 0 mins
Serves: 1

Ingredients

- 1 frozen banana (*as it needs to be cold*)
- 100ml almond or coconut milk
- 1 tbsp honey

Method

Blend everything together until smooth, scoop and enjoy before it melts!

TMH tips why not add a scoop of TMH Pure Vanilla Protein for some extra nutrition

Chocolate Rice Pudding

Prep time: 5 mins
Cooking time: 12 mins
Serves: 2

Ingredients

- 30–40g organic basmati rice per person
- 150ml almond milk
- 1 scoop TMH vanilla protein *(optional)*
- 1 tbsp honey
- 1 tbsp cocoa or cacao powder
- Your favourite toppings from nuts, seeds and fruit – I used a simple raspberry

Method

Wash the rice first, then place in a pan with the almond milk and simmer for 10–12 minutes.

Once cooked, remove from the hob then add the honey, (protein if using), and sieve the cocoa powder in.

Serve in a bowl and top with your favourite toppings.

TMH tips By sieving the cocoa powder it makes it a nice light texture

Paleo Pumpkin Pie

Prep time: 5 mins
Cooking time: 12 mins
Serves: 4

Ingredients

- 1 medium pumpkin *(you will need 16 tbsp of pumpkin puree)*
- 3 eggs *(1 extra egg yolk)*
- 6 tbsp honey
- 360g ground almonds
- ½ tsp cinnamon
- 120g hazelnuts *(or you can use your favourite nut)*
- 1 egg white
- Pinch of sea salt

Method

Cut the pumpkin in half and scoop out the seeds (put the seeds aside to roast later).

Place the pumpkin halves face down onto a roasting tray and fill the base with water, about ½ inch high.

Roast at 180°C for 45 minutes. You are making your own pumpkin puree!

In the meantime make your base. Place your hazelnuts in a blender until they start to bind together, then add those hazelnuts into a mixing bowl with 2 cups of ground almonds, 2 egg whites, pinch of sea salt and mix it into a paste. It needs to be able to stick together. Grease a baking dish with coconut oil, then spoon the base mixture into the dish. Spread it out with your hands and make a slight crust with your knuckles.

Bake the base at 180°C for 20 minutes and once cooked remove from the oven.

Remove the pumpkin from the oven and scoop out 4 cups of the soft pumpkin and blend in a blender until smooth. Now add 1 cup of ground almonds, eggs, honey and cinnamon and blend until thick and creamy, approx. 2 minutes

Remove the base from the oven, allow to cool for 5 minutes, then add the mixture into the dish, make sure it is smooth and bake for 40 minutes.

Cinnamon Roasted Peaches

Prep time: 2 mins
Cooking time: 20 mins
Serves: 2

Ingredients

- 4 peaches
- 1 tsp cinnamon
- 2 tbsp organic butter
- 2 tbsp honey

Method

Cut your peaches in half, remove the stone. Heat a small pan over a low heat and melt the butter, then add the honey and cinnamon. Add the peaches and allow to coat well. Now place the pan in the oven and roast for 15 minutes.

Serve and enjoy.

TMH tips Why not try adding some fresh rosemary, it makes a lovely combination!

Pecan <small>AND</small> Pear Crumble

Prep time: 8 mins
Cooking time: 25 mins
Serves: ?

Ingredients

- 4 ripe pears
- 4 tbsp honey
- 150ml water
- 8 tbsp coconut palm sugar
- 50g gluten-free oats
- 50g gluten-free flour
- 1 tsp cinnamon
- 50g organic butter
- 25g flaked almonds
- 25g pecans

Method

Preheat your oven to 180°C, and grease dish with organic butter. Peel, halve and core the pears, then slice. Layer the pears on the bottom of the dish and pour over the honey and 100ml of water and roast for 10 minutes (this will soften the pears).

In a large bowl mix the gluten-free flour, porridge oats, cinnamon, butter and using your fingers rub together. Now add your pecans and add flaked almonds.

Remove the pears from the oven, now add the crumble mixture on top, and bake for 15–20 minutes.

Homemade Old Fashioned Toffee

Prep time: 5 mins
Cooking time: 15 mins
Serves: 6–8

Ingredients

- 8 tbsp coconut palm sugar
- 1 tsp apple cider vinegar
- 2 tbsp organic butter
- 50ml organic cream
- 3 tbsp honey
- 1 tsp of coconut oil for greasing

Method

In a pan over a medium heat, melt the butter then add the sugar, apple cider vinegar and honey. Keep stirring continuously for approx. 5 minutes. Then add the cream and keep stirring.

To test the consistency of your toffee, you need a bowl of cold water and after approx. 8–10 minutes drop a small amount into the bowl of water and start to mould it with your hands. If it is soft and squidgy then your toffee will be chewy. If you like the harder more traditional toffee then keep cooking until the drops in the water become

Coconut sugar is made in a natural 2-step process: A cut is made on the flower of the coconut palm and the liquid sap is collected into containers. The sap is placed under heat until most of the water has evaporated.

 TMH tips Coconut Palm sugar replicates toffee so well!

hard once you have felt them. Remove from the heat then pour onto a greased baking tray. Place in the fridge and allow to set for at least 30 minutes.

One of my friends smuggled home a jar filled with my homemade toffee, as she loved it so much. Danielle Colley!

Gluten-free Scrumptious Scones

Prep time: 10 mins
Cooking time: 20 mins
Serves: 4–6

Ingredients

- 80g sieved coconut flour
- 1 tbsp tapioca flour *(this makes it chewy)*
- Pinch sea salt
- 3 tbsp coconut butter or oil
- 500ml coconut milk
- 6 eggs

- 100g dried fruit *(optional)*
- 1 tsp vanilla essence
- 1 tsp raw honey

To make the Strawberry Jam

- 500g organic strawberries
- 3 tbsp raw honey

Method

Preheat the oven to 180°C and grease muffin tin with coconut oil.

In a large bowl or food processor, mix the eggs, coconut milk and vanilla first.

Melt the coconut oil first then add this to the mix. Then add the coconut and tapioca flour to the mix.

If you would like to add dried fruit then do so now and combine again.

Place in the muffin tray and bake for 20 minutes.

Jam

To make the jam, place the strawberries in a pan with 2 tbsp of water and allow to simmer and moisten. Place the mixture through a strainer, to remove the pips, then place the mixture back in the pan.

Add the honey, stir and simmer for a few minutes.

Christmas Gingerbread Cookies

Prep time: 10 mins
Cooking time: 30 mins
Serves: 6–8

Perfect for the Festive Parties!

Ingredients

- 225g rice flour *(plus extra for dusting the work top)*
- 125g gram flour *(or chick pea flour)*
- 1 tsp xanthan gum
- 2 tsp ground ginger – or ginger powder
- 1 tsp ground cinnamon

- ½ tsp nutmeg
- 1tsp gluten-free bicarbonate of soda
- 100g organic butter
- 50g coconut palm sugar
- 4 tbsp maple syrup or honey
- 2 eggs
- 100ml almond milk

Method

Preheat the oven to 180°C, then in a food processor combine the flours, xanthan gum, spices and bicarbonate of soda. Whizz the ingredients to mix them thoroughly. Now add the room temperature butter to the processor until the mixture resembles breadcrumbs. Add the coconut sugar and if needed almond milk and mix again.

Now add the maple syrup or honey and eggs and process until the mixture starts to come together. Tip out onto a (rice) floured surface and form the dough into a smooth ball. Wrap in cling film and chill in the fridge for 20 minutes. Take out of the fridge and roll to the thickness of a £1 coin. Using Christmas shaped cutters, start to cut out as many shapes as you can, re-rolling the left overs to use it all up.

Line a baking sheet with non-stick baking parchment and grease with coconut oil, place the shapes on the baking sheet and bake the cookies for approx. 12 minutes until nicely browned but not burnt. Leave to cool on the tray for 5 minutes then transfer to a wire rack to cool completely.

Raw Chocolate Mousse

Prep time: 5 mins
Cooking time: 0 mins
Serves: 1

Ingredients

- 1 avocado
- 1 scoop TMH vanilla protein powder
- 1½ tbsp cocoa powder
- 50ml water or almond milk

Method

Place everything into a blender and blend until smooth, if you want it smoother then just add some more water or almond milk.

Notes...

DRINKS

Fat Flush Water

Prep time: 5 mins
Cooking time: 0
Serves: 3–4

Ingredients

- 1 grapefruit – sliced
- Fresh mint leaves
- 1 lemon – sliced
- ½ cucumber
- 1 lime

Method

Place all the fruit and mint into a jug of cold water and enjoy!

Perfect on a summers day.

Quenching Cranberry

Prep time: 2 mins
Cooking time: 0
Serves: 1–2

Ingredients

- 40ml unsweetened cranberry juice
- 500ml cold water
- Ice cubes

Method

Dilute the cranberry into the water and this will help flush out the liver.

Protein Powder Hot Chocolate

Prep time: 2 mins
Cooking time: 0 mins
Serves: 1

Ingredients

- 1 scoop of TMH vanilla protein powder
- ¼ tsp cocoa powder
- 300ml almond milk

Method

Heat the almond milk in a pan until hot, then in a blender/smoothie maker add the almond milk, protein powder, cocoa powder and blend for 5 seconds.

Pour into a mug and enjoy. If you want a stronger flavour, you can add more cocoa powder.

Chocolate Martini Mocktail

Prep time: 3 mins
Cooking time: 0 mins
Serves: 1

Ingredients

- 150ml coconut milk
- 1 tsp honey
- 1 tsp organic cocoa powder
- Sprig of fresh mint
- Crushed ice

Method

Place the ingredients into a blender and blend until smooth, pour and serve. If you want to make it look a bit fancier, sprinkle some dusted cocoa powder on top.

Cranberry Crush Mocktail

Prep time: 2 mins
Cooking time: 0 mins
Serves: 1

Ingredients

- 200ml coconut water
- 50ml cranberry juice (*I use Biona concentrate*)
- Juice ½ lime
- 4 ice cubes
- 2 mint leaves

Method

Place everything into a blender and blend for 15 seconds, serve in a cocktail glass and enjoy.

Coffee without the Coffee

Prep time: 1 min
Cooking time: 0 mins
Serves: 1

Ingredients

- 1 tsp of ground Yannoh granules
- 200ml hot water
- Dash of almond milk to serve

Method

Add 1 tsp of yannoh into a mug, top up with hot water and add almond milk to serve.

GOOD MOR NING beautiful WORLD

This is a fantastic Natural option when you are looking for a break from coffee, by gently roasting barley* rye*, chicory* acorns* certified organic*

Cleansing Water

To make your H2o a little more interesting try adding some of these lovely fresh ingredients.

Cleanse and Digest
Mint, Cucumber and Lemon

Vitamin C Booster
Orange and Lime

Immune Booster
Ginger and Lemon

Thai Inspired
Lime & Ginger

Mulled Cranberry AND Cinnamon

Prep time: 5 mins
Cooking time: 20 mins
Serves: 3–4

Ingredients

- 1 litre cranberry juice (*dilute Biona cranberry concentrate in water*)
- 2 tbsp raw or organic honey
- 2 cinnamon sticks
- 4 whole cloves
- 1 orange, cut into quarters

Method

Place all the ingredients in a saucepan, then squeeze the oranges to release their juices before placing in pot. Bring to a simmer, cover and gently simmer for 20 minutes to allow time for all the spices to infuse. Strain before serving.

Warm me up!

Chocolate Almond Milk

Prep time: 5 mins
Cooking time: 0 mins
Serves: 2

Ingredients

500ml almond milk
¼ tsp cinnamon
3 tbsp cocoa powder – sieved
1 tbsp honey

Method

Heat the almond milk, cinnamon and cocoa powder in a pan over a medium heat. Lastly add the honey.

Goji, Green and Apple Tea

Prep time: 5 mins
Cooking time: 0 mins
Serves: 2

Ingredients

- 200ml apple juice
- 2 green tea bags
- 200ml water
- Dried goji berries
- ½ tsp cinnamon

Method

Place everything into a saucepan and bring to a simmer, pour into a teapot and enjoy.

I hope you have enjoyed all of my recipes.

Notes...

AFTERWORD

Today's Nutrition
TRULY MADLY HEALTHY
For Tomorrow's Health

Thank you for purchasing my book and I hope you enjoy the recipes!

Jemma x

For more delicious recipes and tips join:

f Facebook page – Truly Madly Healthy

🐦 Follow me on twitter – @JemmaGovier

www.trulymadlyhealthy.co.uk

Featured in

VOGUE BRITISH

pure eat.

NaturalHealth AUSTRALIAN
Health, Happiness & Harmony for Mind, Body & Spirit

Mumazine
for Mums by Mums

EXQUISITE ESSEX
THE ULTIMATE LIFESTYLE GUIDE, EXCLUSIVELY FOR SELECTED GUESTS AND RESIDENTS

INK
Women's Institute New Konnections

Printing: Kestral Printing • **Design & Artwork:** Antony 'H' Haylock & Mark Haylock
Photography: Dean Govier • **Publisher:** Truly Madly Healthy • **Author:** Jemma Sedgwick
First Published: Jan 2015 • Copyright ©Jemma Sedgwick 2015